# FRENCH SCENIC WALLPAPERS

To

EVE

500 COPIES ONLY OF THIS BOOK HAVE BEEN PRINTED

By the same Author

THE BOOK OF WALLPAPER. 1954

A LITERARY HISTORY OF WALLPAPER. 1960

WALLPAPERS OF THE VICTORIAN ERA. 1964

# FRENCH SCENIC WALLPAPERS 1800–1860

by

E. A. Entwisle, F.S.A.

F. LEWIS, PUBLISHERS, LIMITED

Publishers by appointment to the late Queen Mary

LEIGH-ON-SEA

PRINTED AND MADE IN ENGLAND

Copyright by

F. LEWIS, PUBLISHERS, LTD
The Tithe House, 1461 London Road
Leigh-on-Sea

SBN 85317 008 8

*First published* 1972

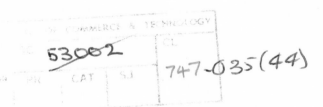
Produced by F. Lewis, Publishers, Ltd
Leigh-on-Sea and printed at the
Daedalus Press, Stoke Ferry, Norfolk
Bound by W. S. Cowell, Ltd, Ipswich

# TABLE OF CONTENTS

(Title page illustration.) Block printer and assistant from F. Follot's *"Causerie sur le Papier Peint"* 1886.

# FOREWORD

THIS BOOK, as its title implies, is specifically concerned with a unique kind of wallpaper which the French manufacturers produced during the first half of the 19th century. They called it "papier peint panoramique", i.e. panoramic wallpaper, or, as we should say, scenic wallpaper.

As will be seen in due course the organisation required to initiate such a form of production was formidable for the wallpaper printing machine had yet to be invented and the complicated scenes portrayed were printed by means of wood blocks each of which had to be "cut" or engraved by experienced craftsmen. Sometimes as many as 3,000 blocks were used to print one set of a particular decoration. In most cases the original panoramic composition was painted by artists who were used to working on a large scale—"paysagistes" they were called, and though they may not have contributed much to the fine arts they certainly re-established the art of the decorative painter in terms of wallpaper, an art which will never be forgotten as long as Michelangelo's paintings on the ceiling of the Sistine Chapel in Rome remain in existence.

Consideration as to the exact origin of the scenic wallpaper is to be found in another part of this book but, bearing in mind the way the artist approached his task, one cannot help comparing his work with that of the scene-painter like, for example, the two Italian painters, Pellegrini and Marco Ricci, who arrived in London during the early part of the 18th century and who were as much at home painting a ceiling in one of the stately mansions belonging to the nobility as in the creation of a theatrical back-drop briefly required for the run of a play. In the main the aim of the decorative painter, the scene-painter and the paysagiste was to create illusion. In this connection one calls to mind William Kent's mural painting in Kensington Palace realistically featuring men, women and children peering out on to the King's Staircase from a trompe-l'oeil balcony, or the animated pictorial scenes painted by Thornhill, Verrio and Laguerre both of whom, in spite of their renown, reflected the humbler art of the scene-painter. (Plate 4).

Of course, these artists, and others like them, were outstanding and expensive to employ seeing that the masterpieces they painted took a considerable time to complete: even Pellegrini, reckoned to be a "prodigious" quick worker, spent many months decorating parts of Castle Howard in Yorkshire, and other mansions in this country and the cost of such work would be proportionately high.

The 18th century saw the best of the decorative painters and while their art was carried on perfunctorily to within recent times, e.g. Rex Whistler, master of decorative illusion, it became necessary, long before this, to adopt other cheaper forms of decoration which is where the French wallpaper manufacturer came into his own: for although the initial cost of producing a scenic wallpaper might be high its reproduction by means of wallpaper printing processes enabled him to recoup this cost, if not show a reasonable profit. Also, with characteristic élan the French maker insisted on the employment of first class artists so that his reputation for quality should be maintained.

Thus the 19th century scenic wallpapers paid off and were, in due course, an object of admiration throughout the western world.

The purpose of this book is to make the story of the French scenic wallpapers more widely known than is the case at present, for even the student of French decorative art is generally unaware of the important part wallpaper—once referred to in this country as the "Cinderella of the applied arts"—has played in this field: certainly he would be unlikely to know the names of the more prominent French makers or the descriptive titles of the special scenic papers they produced.

The following pages may repair some of these deficiencies but, inevitably, such information as they may contain has only been put together after consulting the works of a number of specialist writers on the many aspects of French decorative art. Many of these writers are no longer with us: Henri Clouzot and Charles Follot, for example, and Nancy McClelland of America. The first named author and his collaborateur, Charles Follot, published in Paris, in 1935, the superb volume, *Histoire du Papier Peint* and Nancy McClelland the equally fine book, *Historic Wallpapers*, in 1924. Both these have been specially useful and I have found Sugden and Edmondson's *A History of English Wallpaper* (1926), dependable as ever.

Books on the subject written during the last century have also yielded invaluable information as, for example, Louis Figuier's *Merveilles de l'Industrie* (1878); Sebastien le Normand's *Manuel des Étoffes* (1886) and F. Follot's "Causerie sur le Papier Peint" a lecture given at the Bibliothèque Forney, Paris, also 1886. And it has been impossible to overlook the many articles written during the years, particularly those published in *Country Life* by Ada Leask, the Dublin antiquarian, whose interest in 18th-century English wallpaper, as well as the French product, has resulted in the availability of much dependable material. The many articles in the *Connoisseur* have also repaid close examination.

One of the best known authorities, André Carlhian, died unfortunately before he was able to finalise the results of a life-time's work, but his son, Charles Carlhian, expects soon to arrange for the material to be published.

As for present-day historians I should like to express grateful thanks to M. J-P. Seguin, Conservateur of the Musée de l'Arsenal, Paris, for his kind assistance during my visit last year to the Musée des Arts Décoratifs, and also to Mlle Y. Brunhammer of that Museum, who incidentally collaborated with M. Seguin in the planning and arrangement of that truly spectacular Exhibition of French Wallpaper held there in 1967* the catalogue of which now forms a specially reliable source book. Herr Josef Leiss, director of the Wallpaper Museum at Kassel, and co-author of the recent three-volume history of mural hangings, *Tapeten, Ihre Geschichte Bis Zur Gegenwart* must also be remembered for his ever-willing helpfulness.

In conclusion my thanks are due to those who have shown keen interest in what I have been doing and who have helped in so many different ways: among these I would mention

---

\* Trois Siècles de Papiers Peints. Musée des Arts Décoratifs. Paris. Catalogue of the Exhibition held 22 June–15 October 1967.

my wife for her encouragement; my friend Richard Busby for reading the MS; M. Sangnier for explaining some of the abstruse passages in Le Normand's text book; Mrs Waterhouse of Boston, U.S.A. for her enthusiastic interest; Louis Schreider III for his entertaining notes on Gouverneur Morris; Mrs Catherine Frangiamore of the Cooper-Hewitt Museum, New York; and the staff of the Victoria and Albert Museum Library.

E. A. Entwisle, 1972

# A Few Events in French History

1754–93    Louis XVI.

1789    July 14, The Bastille taken and destroyed.

1789    May 5, States General meets.

1791    Royal family brought by force from Varenne to Paris.

1791    The young Napoleon Bonaparte takes an oath to defend the new regime.

1792    Royal family imprisoned and executed a year later.

1793–4    Reign of Terror—The Guillotine. France at war with most of Europe.

1795–9    The Directory. Government by Committee of Five.

1797    France in the grip of galloping inflation.

1799–1800    Napoleon Bonaparte proclaims himself First Consul.

1804    Napoleon Bonaparte crowned Emperor of France.

1805    Battle of Austerlitz. Austria defeated. Peak of French power.

1814    Emperor Napoleon resigns the Throne. Elba.

1815    Louis XVIII King from this date to his death in 1824.

1815    Napoleon back in Paris.

1815    Battle of Waterloo.

1815    Napoleon on St. Helena.

1821    Death of Napoleon.

1824    Charles X becomes King.

1830    Louis Philippe of Bourbon-Orleans, King of the French.

1848    The year of Revolutions.

1852    Louis Napoleon becomes Emperor Napoleon III.

# I
# The Early French Wallpaper Makers

FRENCH REACTION towards the earliest wallpapers, like that in this country towards our own product, was one of gradual acceptance and, no doubt, satisfaction that a substitute had at last been found for the more elaborate forms of mural decoration which only the well-to-do could afford. Where tapestry, leather and silk, to mention only a few types of hanging in use, once held sway it suddenly became possible to make use of a "hanging" of paper which, surprisingly, possessed almost all the qualities of the fabrics it was intended to imitate. Above all, the new paperhangings were economical to handle and so it comes as no surprise to learn that even the arduous work of the decorative painter was eventually imitated successfully though not by the hard-headed English wallpaper manufacturer whose production routine would not permit any such extravagant experimentation.

It was left to French enterprise to evolve, and reintroduce, the art of the decorative painter in terms of paperhangings and this was done with so much confidence that French scenic wallpapers became as much sought after as the original paintings in many parts of the world, especially in the United States of America. The advent of these scenic papers took place about the time the painter was going out of business, that is to say, about the end of the 18th century and the beginning of the 19th century.

The French wallpaper industry, like that in England, had an interesting history long before the idea of the scenic papers was evolved. As in this country the first paperhangings were produced capriciously by the letter-press printers and the wood-engravers, the "graveurs sur bois", of the Middle Ages, and many of those whose business it was to produce the wood blocks for proclamations, advertisements and even playing cards, often turned their attention to the engraving of blocks intended for more artistic purposes.

The first sheets of decorated papers, measuring only about a foot square, were produced in France towards the end of the 17th century. These were called "domino" papers, a French term for the Italian papers imitating marble, and they were often used not only for the casual decoration of the cottage or small house interior, but also for lining chests and cupboards. The makers of these small sheets, who had already formed themselves into a Guild in 1586, were mainly to be found in Paris and Rouen and were very active up to the middle of the 17th century though at no time did their productions attain the perfection, or the practical usefulness, of those of the true paperhanging maker who was working in France, and here also, towards the end of that century.

Many of the French industrialists who emerged as makers of wallpaper had been in the "indiennage" line of business, i.e. the production of patterned cottons either by painting the design, or printing the material by means of wood blocks. These textiles, or "indiennes",*

---

* "Étoffe de coton, peinte ou imprimée que l'on a fabriquée primitivement dans l'Inde Asiatique", Grand Larousse Encyclopédique.

so named because of their countries of origin, were widely used as mural* and bed hangings as well as dress material, and in view of their popularity those in the industry made great efforts to improve the methods of production. It may well have been that manufacturers began to consider the possibilities of taking up wallpaper printing about the time those in the "indiennage" were experimenting with copper-plate printing, about the middle of the 18th century, but this is conjecture and not, perhaps, a matter that needs to be pursued here.†

No account of the French wallpaper industry would be complete without mentioning the Papillons, father and son, both skilled wood-engravers who carried on business in Paris between 1680 and 1780. It was Jean-Michel Papillon, the son, who is reputed to have engraved his first block, after a design by his father, at the age of nine and who, later in life, earned renown for his text book on the art of wood-engraving published in 1766. It would be possible to devote a whole book to the history of this family for in many ways they were responsible for the foundation of the industry: among them the "invention" of the "repeat" principle and John Michel's contributions to the great Encyclopédie des Science which Diderot took twenty years or more to compile. It is this last which justifies his position as the earliest "historian" of wallpaper since in it he describes, in great detail, its development up to the middle of the 18th century‡

At this period the wide variety of paperhangings available in France, and in other parts of Europe, was quite remarkable. Manufacture was almost wholly confined to hand processes and mainly dependent upon the personal degree of skill possessed by the block-cutter, yet within these limitations the wallpaper maker was versatile to a degree.

The "flock" papers, resembling the Italian cut-velvet hangings (for which invention the French have named, Le François of Rouen, a claim which is contested by those who refer to the Letters Patent granted to Jerome Lanyer, an Englishman, by Charles I in 1634§), were always a popular item and had been since the beginning of the century, and there were also a number of papers imitating wood, marble, and the more common-or-garden floral themes inspired by the old "domino" patterns. Innumerable borders were introduced to enhance the different types of wallpaper "filling". The ways in which these borders were applied were most ingenious; for example, the various panelling schemes obtained with a pilaster-type border, a style of decoration adopted almost universally in England as recently as forty years ago.

In order the better to visualise the versatility of the French wallpaper maker of the 18th century, the following list taken from a dealer's advertisement published in Paris in 1772 is useful. Among the papers in stock are: Landscape papers (paysages); decorations applied over doorways and fireplaces (dessus de portes and devant de cheminées); flock papers (papiers veloutés or papiers tontisse); Chinese and Persian types of design (Indiennes de toutes façons); imitation tiles (carreaux de Fayence); wainscot papers (pour lambris); marble papers

---

* Madame de Pompadour hung with cotton all the walls of the Hermitage at Versailles, c. 1750.
† "En 1686 . . . Louis XIV prohibited the importation and even the manufacture of 'Indiennes'." J-P. Seguin.
‡ Papillon's work and career are fully described in C. C. Oman's *Catalogue of Wallpaper*. A Victoria and Albert Museum publication, 1929.
§ It seems reasonable that the honours should be shared equally by Le François and Lanyer.

(papiers en marbre); wood effects (papiers en écaille); gold finished papers (papiers d'or); floral and bird designs and, of course, imported painted papers from China.

But it was the appearance of the great Jean Baptiste Réveillon, the doyen of wallpaper makers, that added lustre, and new kinds of wallpaper, to the industry.

Réveillon came into prominence during the second half of the 18th century and soon made his mark in Paris as a man of great talent, imagination and taste. The period in which he flourished is usually stated as between 1765 and 1789 but he started his commercial career in 1741 when he became apprenticed to a "mercier-papetier", a sort of general stationer and seller of accessories for women's wear. By 1752 he was the possessor of the lease of a shop selling playing cards and chess pieces and he was also doing business in the then popular imported "papiers bleu d'Angleterre".

Although a number of engravers began to manufacture and deal in wallpaper imitating the English goods Réveillon was by far the most enterprising businessman of them all, and, after running successfully a retail shop specialising in fine wallpaper for a while, he found that he had enough capital to buy, and later convert as a factory, a large mansion in the Faubourg St. Antoine, and a few years later acquired a small paper mill at Courtalin (Seine et Marne), which supplied him with the special paper, of vellum-like quality, which he needed for the superb decorations he was making.★

The large mansion in the Faubourg St Antoine, when equipped with all the block-printing tables and other paraphernalia connected with the manufacture of wallpaper, was capable of accommodating 300 workers and it was here that the beautiful "panneaux arabesques" were produced the designs of which contained elegant ornamentation reminiscent of the decoration seen in the newly discovered cities of Pompéii and Herculaneum. The "panneaux arabesques" were immediately successful for while wealthy people who admired this style of decoration could easily afford to have their walls painted, the introduction of wallpaper of this type made it possible for a much greater number to indulge their taste at less cost (see fig 2 & 60).

It is interesting in passing to mention the fact that Réveillon supplied the paper fabric, in 1783, to Étienne de Montgolfier for the first fire balloon which ascended from the grounds of Réveillon's factory.

There is no doubt that a large measure of the success enjoyed by Réveillon was due to technical efficiency and also to his policy of employing only the finest artists for this special work. In this way he commissioned, among other notable designers who were associated with the Gobelin tapestry works, those who had long experience of designing for the "indien-

---

★ "... Becoming a manufacturer, at the age of thirty, his (Réveillon's) success was unusual at this period. He made use of all the latest developments available in the making of wallpaper; in the use of vellum; the sticking together of sheets to make a roll; block-printing "à la frappe"; employment of the finest colours, etc. He organised his workers into grades according to their ability and offered his wallpapers in various qualities to suit both rich and poor. ("Enfin, il s'appliqua à produire trois sortes de papiers destinés à trois clientèles differèntes; ceux de grand luxe qui pouvaient requérir l'emploi de quelques 80 planches et qui coûtaient aussi cher qu'une tapisserie des Gobelins, des papiers 'communs' à sept ou huit planches pour les bourgeois, et des feuilles très ordinaires, à une seule couleur, à l'usage du populaire.") But above all, he raised the status of the industry by introducing to it the best artists of the period, some of whom were designers for the tapestry industry.

He became noted for the manufacture of papers imitating velvet, damask, silk, printed cottons, wainscotting, etc., and there is only one word to describe these products—enchanting.

The story of Réveillon's success is the more remarkable since others such as, for example, Arthur et Robert, and Jacquemart et Bénard were equally fine makers at this time." *Le Papier Peint en France*, J-P. Seguin, a pamphlet published 1967.

nage" industry: artists like Cietti, Jean-Baptiste Fay, Huet, Lavallée-Poussin, Prieur, Lafosse and Boucher fils, worked for him at some time or another and designed, in addition to the "panneaux arabesques", a wide range of wallpapers which included types such as imitation "Toiles de Jouy", "Toiles de l'Inde", the silk embroideries made in Lyons, and chinoiserie papers in the style of Pillement. (fig. 70)

With so much talent at his disposal it is no surprise to learn that, in 1784, Louis XVI conferred upon him the title "Royal Manufacturer" which recognition was well and truly deserved.

A curious sidelight on the events which followed a few years later is connected with the distinguished American diplomat, Gouverneur Morris, who, on the 27th April 1789 made a visit to a banker of his acquaintance in Paris and was somewhat surprised to find the gates of his premises shut, as were many of the shops in the vicinity. Writing in his diary on that day he records: "There is, it seems, a Riot in Paris and the troops are at work somewhere which has given great alarm to the City. I believe it is *very trifling*".

Besides being the understatement of the century Morris's comment is one of the earliest references to the French Revolution for on the next day, the 28th April, a great mob, goaded by rumours which were completely unfounded, that Réveillon was grossly under-paying his employees, burst into the building in the Faubourg St Antoine and, after destroy-ing much of the contents, set the place on fire.

This tragic event, which Thomas Carlyle described in his magnum opus is considered to have marked the beginning of the Revolution.★ It certainly put a temporary end to the business for Réveillon never fully recovered from the blow and the whole concern was taken over in 1792, by two manufacturers, Jacquemart and Bénard, whose history will be dealt with later on. "La gloire et la richesse de Réveillon sont liés a la qualité de son travail", is how a modern French writer has described this remarkable man who will always be regarded as the maker of some of the most beautiful wallpapers ever produced.

There is some difference of opinion about Réveillon's movements after this disaster but it is known that he appealed for compensation for the loss of his factory to Jacques Necker, the Finance Minister, who granted a renewal of his manufacturers' Warrant—small compensa-tion for the Royal one previously held.

There were, of course, other wallpaper makers during the pre-Revolution period, all worthy of the niches they occupy in the history of the French wallpaper industry, but this is no place to deal with them unless to say that their contributions helped their successors to continue the good work and envisage another form of production—the staggeringly risky

---

★ "The Sieur Réveillon, extensive Paper Manufacturer of the Rue St Antoine, he commonly so punctual, is absent from the Electoral Committee and even will never reappear there. In those immense magazines of velvet paper has aught befallen? Alas yes . . . Was the Sieur Réveillon, once a journeyman, heard to say that a journeyman might live handsomely on fifteen sous a day?" Thomas Carlyle, *The French Revolution*.
"Le pillage d'une fabrique qui honorait Paris et la France tel fut le prélude de la Revolution de 1789" Louis Figuier, *Les Mervéilles de l'Industrie*.

"panoramique" project which, perhaps to their intense surprise (for it could have involved them in catastrophic loss), received widespread acclaim.

The way in which people in England and America praised the scenic papers when, at last, they were put upon the market, was highly gratifying but French artists and manufacturers alike would have been astonished if they had been told that a hundred and fifty years later their products would fetch thousands of pounds at English auctions.

# II

# Origins: Rotondes and the Dioramas

EVERYONE MUST BE AWARE of primitive Man's desire to make a home for himself, and his determination to make that home both comfortable and secure: the urge to decorate, or beautify, his abode was equally strong and as he became more civilised he was able to make use of an increasing number of materials for this purpose such as wood, leather, wool, etc. As the centuries passed, so his decorative instinct became more sophisticated until, at last, he began to consider new materials which called for considerable skill in their production and application—materials like tapestry, silk and velvet, embroidered textiles and decorated leather and paper.

Even in pre-historic times he had delighted in painting the walls of his home, first of all with drawings of the animals and people he had encountered and later, with devices recording the events and progress of the tribe or family leading, eventually, to the development of heraldry and finally to the painting of frescoes.

The sequence of events is part of the story of scenic wallpaper but other significant developments deserve consideration if we are to discover its true origin.

Many people point to the popularity of the painted Chinese wallpapers as being a source of inspiration. In addition to the characteristic floral designs wherein a tall flowering shrub sprang from a base of improbable rocks and balustrades, where exotic birds and butterflies appeared against an egg-shell blue sky, there were other painted papers which depicted the Chinese at work and play taking the form of a non-repeating landscape, with pavilions, paddy fields and pagodas dotted about the overall design. Such papers, which were made specially for the European market, first appeared in England and France during the early part of the 18th century and were truly panoramic: the fact that they became so popular in the Western world may have led the French to embark on their own types of panoramic wallpaper (fig. 1).

Again we are reminded that the French were producing a small version of the scenic variety of wallpaper long before more enterprising makers came on the scene in the first decade of the 19th century, witness the Paris firm, Arthur et Robert, who, since 1772 had been noted for their imitation oil-painted landscapes in printed stucco frames.★

It is really anybody's guess; but before reaching a hasty conclusion it is worth while considering yet another historic phenomenon, quite unconnected with wallpaper that would appear to have suggested the idea of a panoramic decoration capable of reproduction on a practical commercial basis.

---

★ During the late 18th century some French wallpaper makers were producing hand-painted scenic papers. C. C. Oman mentioned a fine example "formerly at Givry, near Verdun, depicting a harbour scene, and showing tricolour flags on some of the buildings, and caps of liberty on the heads of some of the people".

Though it will be outside the recollection of most the Panorama, or as it was often called, the Diorama, was once a well-known form of entertainment in Europe. The Oxford Dictionary describes "panorama" as "a picture of landscape arranged on the inside of a cylindrical surface or successively rolled out before the spectator—a continuous passing scene". This description perfectly fits the particular form of entertainment that went by that name and also, to some extent, the idea behind the panoramic or scenic wallpaper.

At the beginning of the 19th century there were in this country both Panoramas and Dioramas, in the Strand, Leicester Square and Regent's Park, and in Regent Street there was even a Cosmorama! in which visitors (perhaps rather to their consternation), viewed the panoramic scenes through convex lenses giving a splendid effect of reality.★

The Diorama, in Regent's Park, was probably the most elaborate establishment for this kind of thing. Opened in 1823 it had many attractions and refinements which probably accounted for the somewhat high (in those days), prices charged for admission, viz. Boxes 3/–; Pit 2/–. It contained two "picture rooms lighted by windows and skylights in the roof"—an interesting point considering that descriptions of other similar places suggest that the lighting would be artificial.

However, the Regent's Park Diorama was evidently a flourishing concern for in Bohn's "Pictorial Handbook of London", 1854, a fuller description of the place and entertainment is given. It was evidently "situated in a row of fashionable houses turning out of the New Road", and the building consisted of a "Rotunda 40 ft. in diameter so arranged and illuminated as to display by the best effects the changes of light and shade with the greatest accuracy. The accommodation provides for boxes and saloon, the floor of which turns on a pivot for the purpose of bringing the spectator to the subject, like the proscenium of a theatre behind which are the pictures for exhibition."

What fun these Victorians had! There was another Diorama, as stated, in Regent Street, No. 316, to be exact, and this one may have found the competition from the neighbouring establishment something of a strain seeing that the charge for admission to "the very beautiful and much admired lounge" called the Portland Gallery, was only 1/– although for an extra 1/6 one could reserve a seat. Here, what might be termed the "big picture" was advertised as *Views of the Ganges*. The programme was accompanied by a pianist, and a lecturer was at hand to explain the scenes in detail and also to comment on the various animals "exquisitely painted by James Fergusson during a protracted residence in India". This show was put on twice daily at 2.30 p.m. and 7.30 p.m.

To most people these performances had a very special appeal of novelty and this is not altogether surprising seeing that both Panorama and Diorama were forerunners of the "moving" pictures of the 20th century, otherwise known as the cinematograph. They were the first "captive" audiences expectantly sitting in these circular rooms while the exciting unfamiliar scenes revolved about them. No doubt some of them succumbed to the soporific effect of these pictures in the same way as the cinema or television successfully puts many of us to sleep today.

---

★ A "Lampadorama" was advertised in a Paris journal of 1886.

But to return to origins: that great art historian, Henri Clouzot, one time Conservateur of the Musée Galliera in Paris, knew a good deal about the Panoramas in France which he believed were invented before the Revolution and were at least established as entertainments about 1800. He states that two "Rotondes" were opened that year in the Jardin d'Apollon on the Boulevard Montmartre, "qui attirent bientôt tous les curieux" and where was shown, in one of these, views of Paris and, in the other, an imaginative version of the Siege of Toulon.

There may be other scholars who have dealt with this subject in greater depth than M. Clouzot—specialists in the history of the theatre, possibly—but it is unlikely that any will contradict him when he states that such panoramic performances probably inspired a group of wallpaper manufacturers in Mâcon and Rixheim to embark on the manufacture of scenic wallpapers. The names of these manufacturers will be disclosed in the pages which follow but meanwhile it may be of passing interest that in some parts of the world the Panorama still exists. One of these was in operation within recent years, and may still be working, in Waterloo, near Brussels. Well attended by tourists and holiday makers, this circular building contained a vast panoramic painting of the famous battle. Visitors were conducted round a central platform the edge of which was guarded by wooden railings on which they leaned while taking in all the details of the historic scene. When they had absorbed as much of the horrors of war as was good for them they were, of course, herded into another room where military trophies of all kinds were displayed and where souvenirs might be purchased.

The various accounts of the older Panoramas usually omit to mention the additional attraction of a souvenir shop but having seen the well-appointed display in Brussels one feels sure that the advantages of such a scheme would not be lost on either the French or the English exhibitors of the 19th century.

# III

# Characteristics, Methods of Manufacture, Application

IF THE FRENCH AESTHETE showed no great enthusiasm for the scenic wallpapers there was, on the other hand, appreciation from people of taste in other parts of the world: many Americans built their decorative schemes round them and even today one may find, especially in New England, rooms made very beautiful by a panoramic paper put up a hundred and fify years ago.

Let us take a closer look at the principal characteristics of these wallpapers. As already stated the scenic paper was very like a painted wall in appearance especially when produced in grisaille or sepia tints, and to be seen at its best it required to be hung in large lofty rooms uncluttered by tall or bulky furniture such as book cases or cupboards. The scale of the decoration alone was impressive and there was generally a great deal of interest also in the subject matter. The coloured varieties were most attractive and their brilliance remained for a surprisingly long time. The grisaille or sepia versions were placed on the market to suit the taste of those who disliked too much colour on their walls.

Most authorities agree that the average length of the roll was about 8 to 10 ft. long by about 20 in. wide, though even this rough estimate should not be taken too much for granted seeing that reliable experts differ on this point and there might in fact be variations as between set and set.★ What is known, however, is that the manufacturer allowed for plenty of adjustment in hanging, for example, by providing a fair amount of sky in the design which could be trimmed in the case of limited space, or by supplying a large assortment of borders, ornaments or "dado" papers which enlarged the scheme to fit the walls of tall rooms.

The number of lengths, or lés, that went to a complete set also varied from 5 to 10, to as many as 30 lengths or more. Each of these was carefully numbered to indicate the sequence of the panoramic features, and every set was given a title. If the set, as was often the case, was deliberately designed to allow for the display of separate scenes (often panelled as in figs. 14 & 59), then in this case each separate scene was given a title also.

Of little importance to the early 19th century user but extremely useful to the connoisseur of today, is the fact that the original, or early productions, all possessed one significant feature, i.e. a horizontal join at intervals. This is generally difficult to discern when the paper is pasted on the wall because the ground colour is opaque enough to obscure it, but if it is possible to examine the back of the length the presence of the joining is sufficient to indicate

---

★ Figuier and Le Normand mention 8 m. 50 as being the length, which is a little puzzling unless they are referring to the dimensions of ordinary wallpaper.

that the paper was probably printed between 1805 and about 1830. (The joining of small sheets was, of course, unnecessary when "continuous" paper became available.)

As stated, the subject matter of the scenic paper was magnificently various and, indeed, it is difficult sometimes to account for the choice made by the manufacturers. One can appreciate the selection of the classical themes and also the idea behind those papers specially designed for the American market, such as the views of Boston, the Niagara Falls, etc. but the appearance of a paper depicting the adventures of Captain Cook in the South Pacific is a little difficult to understand unless, as will be seen later, its educational value was reckoned to be good for sales. The views of cities and towns were natural subjects for panoramic treatment but the choice of say, "Telemachus in the Island of Calypso", unless considered a winner from a literary point of view, is also somewhat strange. Incidentally, one of the former types, "Les Monuments de Paris" (originally sold at fifty francs in 1814), part of which may be seen in the Victoria and Albert Museum, has a certain historical interest—the statue of the Emperor Napoleon (his abdication took place in that year), has been removed from the chariot on top of the Arc de Carrousel and the soldiers on guard instead of wearing Imperial accoutrements are seen to have the white cockade of the Bourbons (fig. 30).

One use of the scenic paper has not been mentioned, that of pasting it on tall screens. The writer recently came across two large screens, each about 9 ft. high, and each comprising six folds. The scenic wallpaper, depicting rural pursuits, had been specially trimmed and pasted across these folds to form a continuous panorama all along, and at the top and bottom of the screens was pasted a decorative paper border which, unfortunately, had no relationship to the main theme. One hopes that such a deplorable practice as this was unusual but, as will be seen later, it seems that this, and other, unpleasant mutilations were occasionally resorted to.

It may be of interest to explain briefly how these special wallpapers were made. Firstly, there had to be on hand a supply of suitable paper made from the best linen rags to ensure durability. Next the small sheets (as stated the manufacture of paper in continuous lengths had not yet been achieved on a commercial scale), had to be pasted together to form strips of the prescribed length. One practical expert★ has explained that each roll consisted of 24 sheets of about one foot long but it would seem that his reference applies to wallpaper of more ordinary type. Manufacturers may have had to be content also, on occasion with whatever size sheet the papermaker had in stock.

The task of pasting sheets together was usually undertaken by a young girl whose practised hand first gathered together a quantity of sheets and, having arranged a certain number of these in echelon, simply ran over the exposed edges with a large paste brush. When the small sheets were joined together and inspected to make sure the roll was perfect the next process was the grounding of the paper, not, in the first instance, with colour, but with an adhesive called Flanders Glue which evidently served as a base for the subsequent application of the selected ground colour. Very little scientific research has been conducted into the composition of the colours used but it is noticeable that these are, for the most part admirably "fast" in every sense of the word, a remarkable fact considering many of the pigments in those days would not be as dependable as those in use now. The underlying

★ Sebastien Le Normand, *Manuel des Étoffes*, 1886.

medium for all of them would most likely be a form of whiting★ made from china clay or perhaps, in rare cases, the more expensive white lead.

The second grounding process, done with a sweeping motion of the brushes was performed as swiftly as possible so as to avoid the slightest variation in the tint, and after this the surface was expertly brushed in order to make sure that the colour had spread evenly. Both operations took place on long tables so that every length might be fully extended. The workman held a brush in each hand and after completing the brushing he was followed by two young "sweepers" whose task it was to make doubly sure that the surface was well, and evenly, covered.

The grounding processes described were followed similarly for other forms of wallpaper outside the scenic range; for example, some of the co-called satin papers were first grounded with colour and then polished and brushed. Obviously a great deal of care was necessary in this work for it was upon this grounded surface that all the many subsequent colours had to fall, and any imperfection would affect the quality of printing which was such an outstanding feature of these papers. Even so it has been said that a good workman could prepare at least 300 rolls a day if attended by a lively assistant.

The preparation of the blocks was a very important step and these were made in various sizes though never too large as to become unwieldy. They were composed of three layers, applied cross-wise, of which two were generally whitewood and the third sycamore or pear-tree. Because of the fineness of the grain the sycamore or pear-tree wood was the top layer, i.e. the surface which was to be "cut" or engraved. Layering of the wood in this way prevented warping, for the blocks were not only continuously exposed to liquid colour but also had, eventually, to be scrubbed while being cleaned. It is interesting to note that the blocks used today in the printing of high-quality, hand-made, wallpaper are built up in exactly the same way.

The skilled work of "putting-on" to the block by means of tracings, the various outlines and parts of the design, was closely supervised by the designer for it was here, and also in the cutting or engraving, that the "feeling", or the character, of the original design could be made or marred. It has been mentioned before, and probably will be referred to again, that sometimes as many as two to three thousand blocks were needed for each scenic set so it is no wonder that the manufacturing programmes covered such a lengthy period of time.

The actual printing was undertaken by experienced workmen with a practised eye for correct registration. Each block was supplied with pins at the corners and these enabled the printer to apply accurately each successive block so that there was no blurring of the design. It was necessary to have as many different blocks as there were colours, and in case the reader wonders how it was that so many blocks came to be involved, the fact that one single length sometimes required eighty colours which then had to be multiplied by the number of lengths in the set, goes some way towards providing an explanation.

---

★ Distemper, or body, colour is made of whiting finely powdered, soaked in water and well mixed as stiffly as it can be worked and then strained with the proper colours well ground in water. *Magazine of Science*, 1845.

No colour was printed until the preceding impression had dried. This necessity made the acquisition of reasonably large premises essential for as soon as each length received the printing impression it was hoisted away by the printer's boy and hung up to dry. A typical block-printing table of the period is shown on the title page and it will be noticed that a uniform pressure on the block is being applied by a simple lever.

When, at last, all the processes were completed the lengths then had to be numbered, checked, collected into their proper sequence and packed for despatch. If destined for overseas the parcels would be wrapped in tin foil, or similar protective wrapping, to withstand the rigours of a long sea trip. Often enough the complete set would be accompanied by the accessory decorations and these, too, required equally precise handling. It cannot be said with certainty how many people were employed in the various factories at this time,* or exactly how many panoramic sets were produced but one thing is certain, those who worked on these astonishing papers would be unconscious of the fact that in addition to making wallpaper they were also making history.

Compared with most jobs involving the monotonous and highly commercial types of wallpaper regularly handled by the trade the decorator's task in putting up a scenic set must have been quite exciting. Seeing the development of the wonderful panorama as each length went up must have made this work well worth while. In this connection one recalls the comments of an appreciative audience of wallpaper experts who were watching the decorators putting up a small section of a scenic set at an exhibition of wallpaper at Sanderson's London showrooms. As each length was carefully pinned up, (not pasted) for the three or four lengths selected were worth several hundreds of pounds, expressions of admiration were heard on all sides and this exercise revealed very clearly that the spectacular impact of these decorations was at least one of the reasons for their popularity.

It will be shown in a subsequent chapter that the manufacturers used to issue specific instructions respecting their more complicated productions. Both the best known manufacturers, Zuber and Dufour adopted this course and in the case of the latter's "Captain Cook" set, two lengths, Nos. 10 and 11, were specially composed for use between windows and other narrow spaces: there were other similar instances. It seems, however, that these exact instructions were at times disregarded, or not fully understood, and naturally enough there must have been occasions when the decorator had to use his own initiative in rooms of awkward dimensions, often with dire results: one is reminded of the mutilation of many beautiful decorations foolishly pasted on to doors with the intention, one supposes, of retaining the panorama intact whereas the rectangular outline of the door still remained for all to see thus destroying, not only the decorative effect, but also the panoramic illusion which the designer had been at pains to produce.

Mostly, considerable thought was given in the application of these papers which, on the whole, were eminently adaptable. As will be seen Le Normand confirmed this in his *Manuel* by the painstaking use of a reproduction of the scenic set, "La Galerie Mythologique", as well

---

* Réveillon is said to have employed 300 people, see page 13 and Figuier states that in 1860 (about the end of the scenic wallpaper vogue), there were, in Paris, 129 "fabricants" employing 4,459 workers counting 1,600 children under the age of sixteen.

as a number of related borders, as an example of what a decorator might do to adapt this, and other scenics, to rooms of different sizes. This particular set was sold complete with six lengths containing handsome trophies "destinés à rythmer la composition", and this provision would no doubt make the task of hanging easier still. As Le Normand pointed out: "Ces sortes de tentures se prêtent parfaitement pour former des panneaux de toutes les dimensions par la facilité que l'on a de joindre aux sujets ou d'en separer les groupes d'accessoires qui les interrompent".

One last word about hanging concerns the kind of adhesive in use at this time, that is to say if the lengths were not stretched on battens. It must have called for no little experience and a good deal of faith to find a reliable glue or paste that would not spoil these fairly fragile strips of paper. Few writers appear to have investigated this matter very thoroughly probably because they would feel concerned with more important details: but, in fact, much depended on the correct composition and application of the paste. In those days there was no ready-made paste powder to be purchased in neat plastic bags and many an expensive panoramic paper must have been damaged because of ignorance on this score. None was more aware of the importance of properly made paste than the great George Washington who under the heading "Upholsters' Directions", wrote in a notebook in his own hand, ". . . simple paste is sufficient without any other mixture . . . but the Paste must be made of the finest and best flour and free from lumps. The Paste must be made thick and may be thinned by putting water in it." An interesting Decorators' handbook★ of the 1870's, however, deals with this question with still greater clarity and as it seems that the author is describing a practice in universal use for many years it may be assumed to be relevant to the period during which the scenic papers were being used:

"It is found that ordinary flour is the best material for making paste for the use of paperhangers. It is quickly made, as for the purpose of paper-hanging it is not generally boiled. It is made by mixing ordinary flour and a small quantity of alum broken up fine, with a little water out of the chill, and then pouring boiling water slowly in, stirring it well till it thickens. If it is not well stirred when pouring in the boiling water it is likely to be lumpy. If it is too thin, boil it for a few minutes, keeping it well stirred. By covering it up to cool it prevents scumming: or a little cold water thrown on will effect the same purpose. It will be ready for use when it is cold. It should be used rather thin, as the paper is wanted close to the wall which would not be the case if thick paste was used. About the consistency of gruel will answer very well."

This simple recipe was doubtless a well-tried one based on practical experience. An early 18th century wallpaper bill issued by Robert Dunbar of Aldermanbury, contains similar advice in the following words: "make a good stiff paste of the Best Flour and Water".

★ *The Paper Hanger, Painter, Grainer and Decorators' Assistant*, 1879.

# IV
# The Zubers and their Wallpapers

*"C'est Zuber qui exécuta le premier paysage en coloris . . . "*—Figuier.

SOME WRITERS on the subject of 18th century wallpapers have pointed to an Englishman, John Baptist Jackson of Battersea, as being the original innovator, in 1754, of the scenic wallpaper, but have been unable to produce much evidence in support of the claim other than a few small sheets of so-called wallpaper, now to be seen in the British Museum. There appears to be small justification for attributing the idea to Jackson for beyond these sheets which, for the most part, depict rather boring landscapes in which ruined buildings predominate, there is no difference between these small pictures and the many prints to be found in 18th century portfolios. In fact they are not as pleasant as these, seeing that Jackson invariably printed in oil colours which penetrated and stained the paper right through.

Some years ago the American writer, Nancy McClelland, published notes regarding the discovery of what she thought was a Jackson wallpaper in her country but on investigation this proved to be not a printed paper at all but a very elaborate series of decorations painted during the late 18th century by an unknown artist. It would seem that the curious mistique surrounding Jackson's work arises partly from a self-adulatory pamphlet which he published in 1754 announcing the fact that his wallpapers, technically and artistically, surpassed those of all others: yet such is the lack of evidence in the form of actual wallpaper that one begins to wonder whether his productions ever bore any resemblance to the kind of thing we have all been used to regard as such. While a small booklet published in 1752 describing Jackson's work mentions some of his "drawings" as being four feet high it is more than likely that these prints would be used as decorations in conjunction with wallpapered panels.

Very much more solid evidence about the original maker of the scenic papers is available in the case of Jean Zuber, a draper's son, born in Mulhouse, Alsace Lorraine, on the 1st May 1773. Jean Zuber, like most young men of the period, served his usual apprenticeship before joining, in 1791, a firm run by one, George Dollfus, a printer of textiles who started another business eventually which was concerned with making wallpaper. It is obvious that the young man possessed considerable ability and initiative for he was engaged as a traveller for the firm covering, in addition to his native territory, such countries as Italy, Switzerland and Spain. In 1802 he had progressed so well that he became sole proprietor of a wallpaper business in Rixheim which boasted forty-eight block-printing tables, a large number for that time. Unusually rigorous research* into the raw materials used in this form of manufacture resulted almost at once in the production of exceptionally beautiful wallpapers of impeccable

---

* "Ce ne fut pas à Paris mais en Alsace que se réaliserent les innovations les plus utiles dans l'art des papiers peints." Louis Figuier.

colouring and design, so much so that people declared that even the cheapest papers compared favourably with some of the luxurious hangings produced during the reign of Louis XVI.

From the outset it appears that Zuber had the good sense to commission the best designers available, and one of these, J. L. Malaine,* of Mulhouse, before entering the Zuber house had designed for the Gobelin works and also for the well-established wallpaper firm, Arthur et Robert, of Paris, themselves experienced in the production of many kinds of pictorial papers, not exactly scenic in character.

Another gifted designer, Antoine Pierre Mongin who succeeded Malaine, had already made his name as a painter of battle scenes before becoming interested in the proposals concerning the panoramic wallpapers: indeed, for all we know, it may have been Mongin who put the proposals to Zuber, for before very long, there appeared the first of the coloured scenic wallpapers which was called, *Les Vues de Suisse*, the beautiful panoramic scene being made up of 16 lengths. It is on record that Zuber and his designers had already experimented successfully with small landscape effects mostly framed in medallions for the sake of convenience and it may be assumed that that form of production encouraged the pursuit of the panoramic idea on a larger scale.

*Les Vues de Suisse* was launched in 1804, and made a big impression on the trade and the public alike, and when it was exhibited at the Paris Exhibition two years later, the Jury, perhaps recognising the trials which beset wallpaper manufacturers during war-time, awarded the firm a silver medal, the highest award in the Paperhangings Class. The Jury added that in producing this decoration Zuber had overcome great difficulties in a manner which could only advance the progress of wallpaper making.

Mongin produced another remarkable decoration, viz.: *L'Indoustan* (India), in 1807, which, for some reason, seems to have been the last of these major works until the programme was resumed in 1811, with the production of the 20-length set entitled *L'Arcadie*, designed by Mongin again and inspired by Salomon Gessner's poem "Idyllen" written in 1756. This set is believed to have been specially designed for high rooms.

In the meantime, such was the organising ability of the Zuber team that attention was now being given equally to the technical as well as to the artistic side of the business. Particular interest was shown in the preparation of the colours used, and when arrangements were made for the purchase of a paper mill, not far from Rixheim, experiments were started to find a way of producing "endless" paper which everyone knew would do away with the necessity of sticking together all those small sheets and, consequently, revolutionise the industry. In fact those experiments were brought to a successful conclusion in 1830 with the production of a sheet 9 metres long, but by that time steps were being taken in England, with the aid of the Fourdrinier machine, to produce a sheet of paper hundreds of yards long and continue to do so until stopped.

About the same time as *L'Arcadie*, came *Décor a Fables*, containing scenes from the stories

---

*J. L. Malaine, floral painter at the Gobelin factory fled to Mulhouse as a refugee from the Terror. "Les magnifiques reproductions de la nature qui contriburent puissament a fonder la reputation de ce grand établissement." (Zuber).

by La Fontaine, and *Paysage à Fables*, made up of 12 lengths, six of which were made to replace subjects in the "Decor" set.

*L'Helvétie*, came out in 1813–14, and this echoed the theme, or perhaps replaced some of the scenes in the earlier *Vues de Suisse* set.

The painstaking planning for the production of these spectacular wallpapers is evidenced in the amount of time which sometimes separated one series from another: for instance, four years were to elapse before the successor to *L'Helvétie* appeared—this was *Vues d'Italie*,[*] another animated decoration in full colour, consisting of 20 lengths, which was issued in 1818. Next came *Jardins Français*, sometimes known as *le Petit Décor* (fig. 34), a very beautiful theme produced in 1821 and interesting because, in 1836, people dressed in the Directoire style were removed from the design and substituted figures dressed in the style of the day. In 1849 it became *Jardin Espagnol*.

Such after-thoughts were accommodated quite simply for the designer only had to provide for the cutting of new blocks and to instruct the printer exactly where to introduce and print the additional figures, or to arrange for artists to paint them.

*Les Lointains*, a specially lovely landscape decoration, consisting of six lengths, and the last to be designed by Mongin, appeared in 1825 and was followed two years later by a very ambitious set entitled *Vues d'Écosse*, or *La Dame du Lac*, which was produced in 32 lengths, the subject being derived from a sketch by a Parisian artist, J. Michel Gue (1789–1843). An interesting point about this particular set is that it was accompanied by a special Gothic wainscotting paper or dado which lent a splendidly authentic finish. Some idea of its appearance is to be obtained from an illustration in the recently published 3-volume German work *Tapeten*, referred to elsewhere, which shows 14 lengths of the decoration together with the Gothic dado paper.

It is obvious that there were reprintings of this decoration years after its original publication, how many is not known, for at least 12 lengths were until recently in the possession of Messrs Lennox Money Ltd., Pimlico Road, London, S.W.1. Printed on "continuous" paper the lengths measure 7 or 8 ft. long by 18 in. wide (figs. 41–44). The drawing is in the traditional style of the French scenic and two separate shades of grisaille have been used; dark greys for the trees and general landscape, and sepias for the figures. Four lengths of this set were sold at Sothebys in 1968 though the Catalogue attribution to the Paris firm, Mader, remains doubtful.

Another chef d'oeuvre came out in 1827. Designed by Jean Julien Deltil and produced in 30 lengths, it was given the unwieldy title, *Les Vues de la Grèce Moderne ou Les Combats des Grècs*. This was a magnificent battle panorama which made a great impression on visitors to the Exhibition of Wallpapers at the Musée des Arts Décoratifs held in Paris in 1967.

Two more decorations, *Les Vues du Brésil* by Rugendas (fig .40), and *Le Décor Chinois* (figs. 49, 50), followed in 1829 and 1832 respectively, the first consisting of 30 lengths designed by Deltil, the second of 10 lengths designed jointly by Zipelius and Eugene Ehrmann.

If the list of these decorations makes dull reading the same cannot be said of the papers themselves. One can well understand the impact they made on say, the Americans of the

---

[*] which, with additions, painted by hand, became, much later, *Révolution d'Italie*.

early 19th century and one can only admire the enterprise shown by the French, on one occasion at least, in specially catering for this market. Between 1834 and 1836 Zuber produced *Vue de l'Amérique du Nord*, a vast panoramic schema produced in colour and introducing such scenes as a West Point military review, a general view of New York city, a view of Boston and the great Niagara Falls. Delighted with its success Zuber had it redesigned in 1838 and called it *The War of Independence*, the background remaining the same but new figures added to the foreground. It may be of interest to note that in 1969 a somewhat faded set of *l'Amérique du Nord* was put up for auction at Christies and fetched £2,200. This "lot" was described as "An interesting set of French nineteenth century panoramic wallpaper, in fourteen sections, block-printed by Zuber & Cie, Rixheim, Alsace, for the American market, comprising views of American landscapes including Boston harbour, the Niagara Falls from the Canadian side, a military review (possibly at West Point), coaching scenes and Indians; each section approximately 8 ft. high, cut to varying widths, total width approximately 50 ft., *circa* 1840." Christies added that the normal width of a piece of this paper, as originally sold would probably be about 20 in. and also that a similar paper was then to be seen in the Diplomatic Reception Room at the White House. This decoration was found by its makers to be so popular that it was reprinted in 1851, 1854 and as recently as 1913 (figs. 35, 37, 38).

It was not the last of the great masterpieces to be issued by the Zuber factory. The exact number of sets will never be known, but although the founder would no doubt be thinking of handing over the direction to others about this time* there was no lack of additions to the list. For example, there was *Paysage a Chasse* (32 lengths), in 1831; *Courses des Chevaux*, about the same year as *The War of Independence*, which showed racing in Rome, obstacle racing in France and flat racing at Newmarket; and Zuber's sons produced *Isola Bella* (1844), and *Eldorado* (1849), two beautiful floral compositions designed by Ehrmann and Zipelius (fig. 9).

Jean Zuber II died in 1853 of typhoid fever but in 1855 came *Zones Terrestre* (a polar seascape), which Ehrmann designed in colour in 31 lengths.

Bearing in mind the magnitude of these undertakings and the organisation required to see them through it is astonishing to find that all this work represented only a part of the output of the Zuber factory during the period under review.

As has been shown Jean Zuber, from the beginning, had proved himself to be a man of unusual attainments. Not content with the satisfaction of producing wallpapers attractive both in colourings and design he was imaginative enough to improve the many materials, paper, chemicals, pigments etc. which went into the product and also to devise new ways of printing it. Thus, in 1849, the experiments which the firm had been conducting to construct a wallpaper printing machine at last bore fruit and soon after part of the vast production programme was carried out with the aid of machinery.†—"une machine à vapeur et une turbine représentant ensemble une force de 62 chevaux, employés a faire mouvoir 44 machines

---

* In 1835 Zuber père went to live in Mulhouse leaving the business to the second generation, Jean II and Frèderic Zuber.

† "When Ivan Zuber, grandson of Jean Zuber, the elder, founder of the famous house at Rixheim, which claims to have been printing from engraved rollers since 1827, visited this country in 1850 his eyes were opened to the tremendous possibilities of up-to-date machinery. It was from Manchester that he ordered his first steam driven machine." Sugden and Edmondson, *A History of English Wallpaper*, 1926.

servant à la fabrication du papier, a l'impression, au gaufrage, au satinage, etc.", is how a modern French wallpaper historian describes this side of the Zuber activities.

One of the specialities of this firm was the production of small pictorial papers which were used as decorations over doorways and over fireplaces (the "dessus de portes" and "devant de cheminées"). The designers of these smaller pieces were, in some cases, those same people who had excelled in the larger-scale projects, among them, Deltil, Zipelius, Terne, Ehrmann, Fuchs,★ etc. The little scenes were quite charming, as may be seen from (figs. 5, 10, 11, 13). The following titles may be of interest to those who are studying this aspect of decorative art. *Les Quatre Ages*, by Fragnard fils (1810); *Bateau a Vapeur*, by Deltil (1835); *Military Scenes* (1823); *Scotch Scenes* (1827); *Greek Subjects* (1828); *Lake George and Hudson* (1833); *Maison Bernoise*, by Deltil (1835); *Départ en tournée de J. Zuber fils*, by Ehrmann (1835) and *Les Moutons et l'Orage*, by Eberle (1860–62).

Some fine examples of Zuber's wallpaper output during the early part of the 19th century were exhibited at the 1967 Exhibition at the Musée des Arts Décoratifs, Paris, included among which were many of the more usual repeat-pattern papers exquisitely coloured and printed. One of these had a rainbow ground (irisée), and another its foliage printed in green flock: other designs were printed on satin grounds producing the richest possible effect. The portrait of the *Empress Eugenie*, en grisaille, surrounded by a framework of perfectly drawn flowers (fig. 69), was produced by Zuber et Cie in 1865 and demonstrates well the quality of the workmanship at this time.

The foregoing notes on this firm's productions do not, of course, cover all the types of wallpaper marketed, and it may be that the list of scenic wallpapers falls short of some titles, but it interesting to note that some of those mentioned are still being printed by Zuber et Cie from the original blocks and that the agency for them is held by the London firm, Cole &Sons (Wallpapers) Ltd.

---

★ Madeleine, "of the Gobelins" is mentioned by F. Follot and N. McClelland mentions Mongin and Rugendas.

# V

# Joseph Dufour and Amable Leroy

THE CURRENT Dictionary of French Biography,[*] in process of compilation, is sufficiently advanced, at least, to include the name of Dufour. Eventually the names of two more French wallpaper manufacturers should undoubtedly appear, viz. Réveillon and Zuber, and if so these three will surely receive the posthumous accolade they so richly deserve.

The dictionary which will presumably equal in importance our own Dictionary of National Biography, is a little uncertain in its reference to Dufour because in claiming this wallpaper manufacturer to be second only to Réveillon, "après Réveillon il peut-être considéré comme le créateur de l'industrie du papier peint", it overlooks the important parts played by Arthur et Robert, Jacquemart et Bénard (fig. 41), and also Zuber, who many would consider to have shared with Dufour the "invention" of the scenic wallpaper. It is also rather extraordinary that the biographers should have been so arbitrary in the listing of the latter's scenic productions. The magnificent scenic set known as *Les Amours de Psyche* which Dufour produced in 1816 and which is regarded as his masterpiece, figures last but one in the list and is referred to simply as *Le Bain de Psyche* although this, in fact, is the title of only one tableau among the twelve of which the set is composed.

Nevertheless, to be included in a work of such magnitude and importance is proof of Dufour's commercial status and artistic sensibility, qualities which are born out by the comments of those who knew him, especially in the memoir published by Sebastien Le Normand shortly after Dufour's death. (See Comments Chapter.)

Joseph Dufour, like Réveillon, was a wallpaper enthusiast, and though his father, a carpenter, seems to have had small interest in his son's special leaning he may well have shared some of the responsibilities of the business which was being run, in 1790, in the Rue de la Paroisse at Mâcon, under the style, Joseph Dufour et Cie.

It is interesting, in passing, to speculate about the family's experiences during the all too recent horrors of the Revolution since at least two wallpaper makers, René Grenard and Arthur of Arthur et Robert, were guillotined, but it would appear that all survived safely.

Joseph Dufour was born in 1752 and was the father of two children, a boy and a girl when, in 1808, he opened his wallpaper factory in Paris in the Rue Beauvau. The building, which stood in the grounds of the ancient Abbey St Antoine, offered employment for two or three hundred workpeople some of whom, if they followed their "patron" to his new quarters, would be experienced craftsmen versed in the technique of scenic wallpaper production seeing that they must have been present when the famous Captain Cook wallpaper was

---

[*] *Dictionnaire de Biographie Française* (1967–).

being planned. Some of them would also remember making other interesting, even exciting, wallpapers, "nouveautés" as they were called, especially the "drapery" papers and the pretty figures in Evariste Fragonard's panels, *Les Mois de l'Année* (fig. 15), which were produced in grisaille and were no doubt among the first semi-scenic decorations to be marketed by Dufour. It is not known exactly when this set, consisting of twelve lengths, was planned but it would appear likely that the first full-blooded scenic paper from this factory, viz. *Les Sauvages de la Mer Pacifique* (The Voyages of Captain Cook), was being compiled about the same time. It was printed at Mâcon under Dufour's personal supervision, from gouache cartoons painted by the very competent artist Jean Gabriel Charvet, and the 20 lengths, each about 20 in. wide, extended when hung side by side, to roughly 34 ft. (fig. 16).

In an accompanying leaflet Dufour explained some of the difficulties that might be encountered in hanging the decoration and expatiated on his manner of arranging the lengths to fit any available space. Also he went on to describe an unexpected quality which this wallpaper possessed, viz. an educational value in the flora and fauna to be found in the varied scenes portrayed. Children, he believed, would find botany, for instance, more easily understandable by studying the different plants shown.★

When this paper came out it was not regarded too favourably, those concerned obviously being unable to appreciate wallpapers of such unusual appearance and peculiar dimensions. Even Charvet, the designer, was regarded with some indifference.

Setting a fashion which other manufacturers of scenic papers were quick to follow, Dufour numbered each length and named the different scenes or tableaux which the decoration contained. The practicality of this system enabled the decorator to select any scene he thought suitable for his purpose and then the chosen lengths were framed with a paper border supplied by the manufacturer. Most of the named scenes in the Captain Cook wallpaper were confined to one length but this did not prevent the decorator from combining more than one scene in his panelling scheme if he thought fit.

Anyone who has seen this remarkable decoration will marvel at the way in which the operation was organised. There is no doubt that all the careful work involved proved worth while for it is said that Dufour's move to Paris was decided upon because of the success of the undertaking.

But when Dufour left Mâcon he also left behind the talented designer Charvet and it was only by chance that he met in Paris another artist of equal distinction, Xavier Mader, who was to work closely with the Dufour group for the next fifteen years. Mader, before embarking on his wallpaper career had designed for, and learnt the art of engraving in, the "indiennage", at Nantes, and so he was familiar with the very similar procedures involved in making wallpaper.

Mader and Dufour first produced a decoration containing sixteen "figures" called, *Portiques d'Athènes* (fig. 51) and also two very important projects were undertaken, viz. *Galeries Mythologique* and *Les Monuments de Paris* (figs. 18, 30), both of which decorations appeared in 1814 but must have occupied years in preparation.

---

★ In this leaflet, issued in 1804, Dufour states: " . . . Une mère de famille donnera des leçons d'histoire et de geographie a une petite fille vive. Les végétaux mêmes pourrant servir d'introduction a l'histoire des plantes . . . " etc.

The *Galeries Mythologique* (fig. 18), was described in Le Normand's *Manuel* of 1856 where the author showed, at some length, methods of fitting the sheets and surrounding borders to

the shapes of various rooms. It was composed of 24 lengths and the figures were in grisaille heightened with green and blue colours. There were six complete scenes in the set added to which were supplementary sheets containing trophies etc., which could be used in conjunction as desired (see diagram above).

*Les Monuments de Paris* (figs. 30, 31, 32), was different from most of the other scenics in that it was more truly panoramic. This paper was produced in 30 lengths in colour and featured many famous buildings including the Palais de Tuileries, Arc de Carrousel, Palais Mazarin, Notre Dame, Place et Colonne Vendôme, Les Invalides and Palais du Luxembourg. None of these buildings appeared in its correct position visually, this requirement being sacrificed to artistic expediency. Delightfully unusual this production, however, lacks some of the pictorial charm of other compositions; for example, it was certainly not to be compared with the wonderful decoration on which Dufour's fame undoubtedly rests, viz. *Les Amours de Psyche*. This consisted of 26 lengths about 20 in. wide by 5 ft. 7 in. long. About 1,250 blocks were used in its production and the set was issued in both grisaille and sepia, though the latter is rare. The date of manufacture in this case is authenticated by a note found on one of the panels, i.e. ''This paper was invented by Joseph Dufour in the year 1816''. The designer was Louis Laffitte, an historical painter of consequence[*] who composed this decoration in such a way as to provide for twelve tableaux which were sometimes placed separately in panels and framed with a suitable border (figs. 20-24).

---

[*] Louis Laffitte, "dessinateur du Cabinet du Roi, 1770–1828. Premier Grand Prix de Rome, 1791".

Nobody seems to know how long it took to prepare this great set but most experts consider that, like the earlier examples referred to, it would be no exaggeration to say that many years may have passed even before the blocks were ready for the printers: in fact, it looks as if the block-cutters may have undertaken work on at least three different scenic papers at one and the same time.

It is possible that the *Psyche* set, or part of it, will have been seen by more people than is the case with any other scenic wallpaper. A number of lengths was exhibited at Sanderson's Berners Street Showrooms in 1937 and also in 1967 and four lengths adorned, for a number of years, the writer's office in Mortimer Street, London. A section of this paper is still to be seen on the North Staircase of the Victoria and Albert Museum, South Kensington, where it has been for many years. To the uninitiated the beautifully printed classical figures look exactly like painted ones and even on close inspection the perfect registration of the numerous tints, darks first followed by each successive print until the highlights were applied, seems quite incredible. There is reason to believe that Laffitte was unable to undertake all the work involved and that an artist named Blondel* shared some of the design with him. The cartoons were originally drawn and painted on a small scale and finally were enlarged in the printing without loss of grace or quality. Mader is said to have supervised the engraving of the blocks in this case.

The *Psyche* set was so successful that it was sold all over the world and was reprinted several times.

Between 1816 and 1820 Dufour and those of his staff connected with this type of production rested on their success, but between 1821 and 1828 at least a dozen sets, or "suites" as they were sometimes called, followed requiring the preparation of between 15–20,000 blocks. This plan of advance preparation served Dufour in good stead for Xavier Mader left the firm in 1821 and started business on his own account which, as it happens, was the modest beginning of another well-known firm, Desfosse, which will be mentioned in another chapter.

Some of the decorations which Dufour worked on during the years of preparation are listed below: *Les Vues d'Italie*, or The Bay of Naples set was produced in 1822–3 and consisted of 33 lengths printed not in full colour but in monochrome tints such as sepia, mauve, bistre and grisaille. The planning and production of this set, whose artist seems to be unknown, must have occupied some considerable time for included in the panoramic scenes are Tivoli, Amalfi, the Bay of Naples seen from the shore with ships at anchor and also Vesuvius in eruption (figs. 52, 53, 54).

Notwithstanding the detailed nature of the composition the complete set was sold for only 25 francs thus ranking among the cheaper of Dufour's monochrome decorations. Although its cheapness would ensure its popularity it is rarely found today in its complete form. Records show that out of 15 to 20 cases where it has been found in American houses in very few of these is the set complete, and even in France it is the same story. It is almost certain that panoramic views of Italy were featured in the Boulevard Montmarte booths

---

* Méry-Joseph Blondel (1781–1853), pupil of Regnard; Prix de Rome, 1803. Décorateur officiel des Palais de la Couronne sous Louis Philippe.

36

at the beginning of the century and that Dufour was inspired to repeat this subject in wallpaper.

Nearly every wallpaper historian has drawn attention to this example in one way and another and none in a more entrancing manner than Kate Sanborn who, in her book, *Old Time Wallpapers*, published in 1905, described her early recollections of the wallpaper: "For although a native of New Hampshire", she wrote, "I was born at the foot of Mount Vesuvius and there was a merry dance to the music of mandolin and tambourine round the tomb of Vergil on my natal morn. Some men were fishing, others bringing in the catch; further on was a picnic party, sentimental youths and maidens eating comfits and dainties to the tender note of a flute; and old Vesuvius was smoking violently. All this because the room in which I made my début was adorned with a landscape, or scenic wallpaper."

*Paul et Virginie*, was a fine monochrome production illustrating incidents from the love story by Bernadin de Saint-Pierre.* The artist was Jean Broc who split up the story into eight parts: (1) The Slaves bringing Paul and Virginia on a Litter; (2) Domingo and his dog discovering the lost children; (3) Virginia obtains a Pardon for a runaway Slave; (4) The children Dance; (5) Last meeting between Paul and Virginia; (6) Paul and Domingo in the Chapel; (7) Shipwreck and Death of Virginia; and (8) Discovery of the body of Virginia.

This large set was completed in 1823 and put on sale the following year. It was an exceedingly popular decoration and numerous printings went to America.

Mader was the sole author of the next set from the house of Dufour: *Les Fêtes Grecques*, which was printed in grisaille and issued in 10 lengths. Then came *Les Paysages de Télémaque* (fig. 28/29), which, in Balzac's opinion was "un décor démodé" but which everyone else considered to be nothing short of marvellous. The identity of the artist is in doubt, even unknown perhaps, but there is no question about this being another of Dufour's great masterpieces. It came out between 1823 and 1825 in 25 lengths and 2,027 blocks were cut and 85 different colours employed.

An interesting article appeared many years ago in the *Connoisseur* in which the author, Ewart Dudley, described part of a set of 'Télémaque' found in Fairlie House, Ayrshire. Because of its great interest and its value, not to say elegance, each length was carefully removed, and after restoration, mounted on plywood and rehung in a house in London. Apart from a somewhat heightened colour range, the decoration was said to have suffered no damage whatever and, unless something untoward has happened, it will probably be still giving its present owner a lot of pleasure.

The story on which this paper is based is the search for Ulysees by his son Telemachus which legend was described in a book published by François Fénelon, Archbishop of Cambrai, in 1699. The characters appear in classical garb, the gracefully flowing robes being seen to advantage against a background of tranquil skies and luxuriant vegetation. Although one of the most beautiful of the Dufour decorations this is not the most rare, many examples being recorded in America sometimes mixed up with lengths taken from the Bay of Naples set described above.

---

* An informative well-illustrated article dealing with this set appeared in the November 1964 issue of the Norwegian magazine *Tapet-Nytt* viz.: "Tapet, med Romantiskt Litterärt Motiv" by Gunnar Tilander.

*Les Incas* (figs. 25-27), was produced about 1826 and once again over 2,000 blocks were used to print the 25 lengths. The colourful scenes were inspired by a book describing the Conquest of Peru by Pizarro in 1531: the set was sub-titled "The Destruction of the Peruvian Empire". The dignified, but stylised, natives in their impressive finery accord well with a background of volcanic mountains and tropical foliage. This spectacular paper must have been very popular in view of the number of times it has been found in various parts of the world.

*Les Voyages d'Anthénor*, consisting of 25 lengths, in colour, was issued in 1827* and owed its subject to a book published in 1798 in which Anthénor, the hero, is seen journeying in Greece and in Asia. Some of the scenes from this set were occasionally used in combination with the Telemachus paper.

It will be noticed that some of these decorations derived their subjects from literary sources and the splendid *Renaud et Armide* set was no exception. All the 32 lengths were printed in 71 vivid colours and 2,386 blocks were used in the complete production. It was inspired by a poem "Jerusalem Delivered", by Tasse the 16th-century Italian poet, and was printed for the first time in 1828. It has a special interest because although not actually put on the market until 1831 it was the last scenic wallpaper planned by Dufour, the great man having died in 1827.† The set was made up into the following scenes: (*a*) Tombeau de Clorinde et Camp des Croisés, Les 1–6; (*b*) Prodigues de la Forêt Enchantée, Lés 7 et 8; (*c*) Paysage inter-médiaire, Lés 13 et 14; (*d*) Renaud s'embarque avec ses compagnons, Lés 17–21; (*e*) Renaud triomphe des démons d'Armide grâce à son épée enchantée, Lés 22–24; (*f*) Combat de Renaud et de Soliman et Triomphe des Croisés, Lés 26–32 (fig.19).

Dufour had two children, as we have said, but it has not been mentioned that the girl became the wife, in 1821, of a man who, some time before he became interested in wallpaper, was already becoming of consequence in public affairs. This man was Amable Leroy, son of a notable Lyonnais. Amable, a commander of the Garde Nationale and a member of the Légion d'Honneur, took control of the business on the death of his "patron".

Having been born in 1788 Amable was approaching middle age when he assumed these responsibilities, but he seems to have settled down to the situation and fulfilled all expecta-tions without interrupting normal production programmes: in fact, he alone was responsible, in 1829, for another fine decoration entitled, *Les Campagnes des Armées Françaises en Italie*, this time printed in grisaille. The animated scenes covered an area of nearly 50 feet and one can follow the campaign from the Passage over the Alps to the capture of Naples.

Another complete set for the year 1829 was *Les Rives du Bosphore*, although it would appear that this theme was first tried out as early as 1815.

The Dufour–Leroy firm produced many more panoramic papers than those described, for one finds among the notes of wallpaper historians passing references, sometimes a little hesitant, to certain papers which, although not definitely ascribed to Dufour, bear the stamp, figuratively speaking, of the Dufour team. In this connection it is interesting to refer to the

---

* In the Catalogue of the Sanderson Exhibition of 1937 André Carlhian put the date as "about 1825".

† "Cette suite est sans doute la dernière a laquelle Dufour ait donné ses soins." Catalogue of the Exhibition, "Trois Siècles de Papier Peint", at the Musée des Arts Décoratifs, Paris, 1967.

list of designers and technicians which F. Follot gave in his 1886 lecture since it is probably the first time the names of the artisan-type of employee has been recorded by the employer. Laffitte, designer to the King, Mader père, Lapeyre, Portelet, Wagner are mentioned among the designers (and in addition there were Charvet and Broc, already given above); and among the employees are, the engravers, Leger, Dumont, Lemaire et Laffineur; and foremen Bouton père, Hans and Rubie.

It may also be useful to add some of the sets attributed to this firm though not very much is known about them. One such decoration full of interest and elegantly costumed Eastern figures, which Ada K. Longfield (Mrs Ada Leask), illustrated in *Country Life* (15th March 1956), was discovered by the late André Carlhian and given a provisional title by him, viz.: *L'Ouverture des Détroits*. He suggested the date of its manufacture as about 1820–25, and the number of lengths to be at least thirty.

*Les Français en Egypte* (figs. 36, 39), is another colourful and well-planned scene, probably designed by Deltil about 1814. *Paysage Turc, Paysage Décor, Olympic Fêtes, Views of Lyons, Views of London, Paysage Indien,* and *Paysage Pittoresque* are all considered to be Dufour titles as also is *Le Cid*, another interesting paper subsequent printings of which reveal different figures appropriate to the periods in question. A Dufour production *Vue de L'Inde* is shown (fig. 33) this was produced in 25 lengths, about 1815, and was re-edited as *Paysage Indien*.

Finally, it is known for certain that Dufour–Leroy produced a number of minor scenic-type papers some of which are taken from Boilly prints and these, no doubt, would augment the variety of over-door decorations and chimney-breast papers which we know to have been in great demand. *Vue d'Hereford*, a "devant de Cheminée" panel, was produced by Amable Leroy in 1828.

# VI

# Jacquemart et Bénard and Other Makers

ALTHOUGH THE STORY and the achievements of both Dufour and Zuber are eventful in every sense of the word the history of Jacquemart et Bénard is at least as interesting as either.

Pierre Jacquemart, son of a notary had, since 1762, run a business dealing in painted linens (l'indiennage again), in the Rue St Merry in Paris. He came into prominence as a wallpaper manufacturer when, in 1791, he and Eugène Bénard,* a "chef du contentieux", took over the lease of Réveillon's factory in the Faubourg St Antoine. It will be recalled that these premises were pillaged and burnt by a Paris mob in 1789 but it appears that although considerable damage was done to the contents a good deal was left unspoiled or capable of being salvaged. Because of this, no doubt, many of the valuable blocks and printing paraphernalia which had helped to establish Réveillon's fame as a maker of fine quality paperhangings would come into the possession of the two partners and it was this that probably persuaded them, in 1792, to buy the business outright, and benefiting not only from the varied quantity of designs but also from the notoriety of the great man they easily revived old associations and cultivated a new clientele into the bargain.†

In some respects the Revolution was not completely disastrous for them: as a result of this upheaval the necessity of keeping buildings in good repair, both inside and out, had been neglected and this applied as much to the government offices as to less important property. The new heads of state, glowing with Republican fervour, naturally encouraged the use of the now popular Republican emblems in the design of architectural ornament and in textiles and wallpaper, and so the welcome flood of contracts which Jacquemart et Bénard received was invariably concerned with wallpapers whose designs contained a liberal scattering of cockades, Caps of Liberty (Phrygian bonnets), and tri-coloured ribbons fig. 7).

This trend in wallpaper design must have been very marked for there is a record of a firm in the Place du Carrousel at this time which made nothing else but wallpapers of this kind even though one of the partners had fallen a victim of the guillotine.

It was essential to keep abreast of the changing times and this is borne out by the fact that manufacturers of decorative goods might find themselves on one occasion introducing the coq Gaulois and the words "Liberté, Egalité, Fraternité" into a design and on another featuring the fleur-de-lys motif and the inscription, "Vive le Roi". Like the Vicar of Bray the wallpaper manufacturer in France had to trim his sails to whatever breeze was blowing

---

* His full name was Eugène Balthazar Crescent Bénard de Moussinières.

† It seems clear from Gouverneur Morris's diary (see page 14) that although Jacquemart et Bénard were now the proprietors of the factory in the Faubourg St Antoine, people still looked upon it as the Réveillon works. On the 19th June 1792 Morris writes "... Then to Réveillon's paper manufactory to purchase some hangings for Mrs Morris".

and this, like most other things, he did superbly well. The wallpaper which featured the Gallic cock, with its flamboyant, outspread wings was, so it is said, the most popular wallpaper of the period and it was used in all the Paris clubs as well as in lesser buildings.

But nothing is perfect, and designs calculated to meet a momentary fancy will not keep a wallpaper factory running profitably: it is still more difficult to keep it going if these goods are not paid for. Governments are notoriously careless about meeting the bills occasioned by their dubious activities and at least this was true of the governments during the period of Jacquemart and Bénard's business life. These two industrious men, their top artists and their 250 employees, might be building up a reputation for colourful patriotic wallpapers but it was extremely disappointing to find that the response to their efforts was confined to admiration alone.

When Pierre Jacquemart died, in 1804, he left three sons one of which, Auguste, took his father's place as associate of Bénard. He had all his father's business talent as well as an enlightened attitude towards design.

Following the award of a silver medal at the Paris Exhibition of 1806 Auguste was busy on important contracts for decorative work in the palaces of Fontainebleau, St Cloud and the Tuileries but, in spite of the prestige which such work brought, the regrettable fact remains that, because the authorities refused to settle his accounts, he was forced to beg financial assistance. It is a tribute to this man's character that, not only did he continue to make fine wallpaper but he earned eventually as great a reputation for taste and discernment in design as Réveillon had before him.

One of the great scenic productions undertaken by this firm was the magnificent set entitled, *La Chasse de Compiègne* which came out about 1816. As its title implies this decoration depicts a hunt and the setting in the French countryside is filled with scores of horsemen and women elegantly attired in hunting pink, together with retainers, onlookers and animals. The first six or seven lengths show the members of the hunt about to move off from in front of a large mansion and the following six lengths reveal a dozen or so riders approaching a river, the hounds in full cry. The mansion is no doubt intended to be the Château de Compiègne.

This is a highly dramatic, as well as an unusually decorative set for in the next six lengths a noble stag (for that is what is being hunted), has plunged into the river only to be seized and killed by the hounds on reaching the opposite bank. The last lengths show the hunting party taking refreshment while resting from their exertions.

The scenery, the beautiful trees and the placid summer sky, the many figures peopling this decoration have been exquisitely portrayed by the artist, Charles or Carle Vernet, the historical painter (1758–1836). It is the only true scenic wallpaper to have been produced by this firm yet many have considered it finer than any other, not excepting those made by Zuber or Dufour. Consisting of 25 lengths, in full colour, this set called for the use of more than 3,000 blocks (fig. 64).

The Sanderson Catalogue of the André Carlhian Exhibition of 1937 includes this interesting note on the "Chasse de Compiègne" decoration:
"There are two different renderings, the older in which the huntsmen wear red coats, the huntswomen are in red costumes, and servants in blue; in the second rendering the

huntsmen wear blue coats, the huntswomen are in grey costumes, and the servants in red.

"On comparing them it will be noticed that the red and white saddle cloths which are in the older edition have not been corrected in some parts of the second rendering.

"This paper is remarkable in many ways, notably for the precision of the costumes and details, such as carriages, harness, trumpets, hunting horns, knives, etc.

"Contrary to previous opinion, the red coat was not that of the first Napoleon, who hunted in green, but that of the Marquis de l'Aigle, who hunted in the forest of Compiègne. The blue costume, being that of Orléans, indicates that the restoration of Louis XVIII was the reason for the change of colour. The scenes from left to right are first, the departure for the hunt from the Château de Compiègne, of which the facade and railings can be recognised. On the flight of steps the small personage in blue coat would have originally represented Napoleon I. The hunt proceeding toward the right is terminated by a flourish of the horn and the hunters' meal.

"A set of this paper is owned by Lord Ravensworth at Eslington Park, another by Lady Horner, a third by Mr Horace More, New Berlin, New York, and another by Mr John Albion, Andrew House, Salem, Massachusetts.

"This paper is considered to represent wallpaper at its zenith in the matters of elaborate composition and fine printing . . ."

Some idea of this firm's considerable range of production was revealed at the 1967 Exhibition held at the Musée des Arts Décoratifs. Here displayed in orderly profusion were many designs and projects for wallpaper drawn at the end of the 18th century, some of which bore the artists' instructions to the printers and colour mixers, etc. Also displayed were several original designs and wallpapers of the 19th century.

In 1836 Auguste handed over the business to his younger brother, René, and not long afterwards the firm, still retaining its policy of perfection, was obliged to close down for no other reason than that it could not compete with other makers who offered similar goods at very much more acceptable prices.

It will be useful, perhaps, briefly to refer to other wallpapers produced by Jacquemart et Bénard. One set of 30 lengths, in grisaille, entitled *Quatre Saisons* was put out between 1800 and 1810 and, according to André Carlhian, was somewhat similar to *La Chasse de Compiègne*. There was, too, an elegant decoration, *Le Parc Français* which Henri Clouzot attributed to the firm.

Another maker of fine scenic wallpapers deserving of mention is Desfossé et Karth. The beginnings of this firm may also be traced to the 18th century and to Nantes where, as already stated, the Maders, father and son, were conducting a business which specialised in the preparation of the wood blocks and copper plates used in the cotton and linen printing industries. Xavier Mader, the son, entered the Dufour factory as a designer in 1814 (see Dufour Chapter), where he remained for several years until eventually leaving to start a business on his own. After his death in 1830 his widow and her two sons carried on until 1851 at which date one Jules Desfossé took over.

But before Desfossé came on the scene the house of Mader was producing fine wallpapers included among which was the remarkable "plafond" or ceiling decoration entitled *La Toilette de Venus* which appeared about 1814. Le Normand in his *Manuel* attributes this rare

43

ceiling paper to Joseph Dufour, but however this may be, the ingenious way in which its application could be adjusted to suit any size of ceiling is worthy of mention especially since Le Normand, as in the case of the "Galeries Mythologique", supplied a carefully drawn diagram to illustrate the procedure (Page 35). There were, also, *Le Décor Franc Macon* and *La Galerie Poetique* which were reprinted by Desfossé who, during the 50's, concentrated on three spectacular "grands décors" different from the true panoramic type in that they were devised and painted by Charles Muller who specialised in designing floral wallpapers. Some critics have denounced Muller's wallpaper work because of its imitativeness but the beauty and impressive character of two great compositions cannot be denied. They were, *Le Jardin d'Hiver* (1853), and *Le Jardin d'Armide* (1854) (fig. 57).★ The latter was displayed in all its glory at the 1967 Exhibition in Paris and the effect of the massed flowers and foliage, as well as the accompanying side panels and elaborate borders, was truly astonishing: but, of course, where could such an awesome and overwhelming decoration have been used today without it being considered a little provocative? *Le Jardin d'Hiver* (fig. 58), was just such another trompe-l'oeil masterpiece though rather more formal in treatment. *Galerie de Flore*, produced in 1856, was another Muller creation consisting of four main subjects and two accessory vases together with special border and frieze.

*Le Rêve de Bonheur* was designed by an artist named Durrant. Composed of 16 lengths, it was produced in 1852. The elaborate arrangement shown in the illustration (fig. 55), is achieved by "framing" the main tableau with the pilasters and borders designed for the purpose—a regular procedure adopted by Desfossé who, in this way, brought into prominence very conveniently the decorator-paperhangers who were eager enough to assume credit for the panels which belonged to the manufacturer and to no one else.

Other interesting items attributed to Desfossé et Karth are: *Monuments de Paris* (1857), a series of four views in gold frames, viz. L'Obélisque de Luxor, Saint Sulpice, La Porte Saint-Denis and La Tour Saint-Jacques. The illustration (fig. 59), shows these panels hung in company with a fine pilaster decoration and borders which were printed by Gillou et Thorailler, in 1867, and called, *Décor Neo-Grec*. There were also, *Paysage or Panorama Chinois*, *L'Eden* (1860) (fig. 56), *Les Saisons des Fleurs*, *Le Brésil*, *Paysage Exotique* (perhaps part of *Le Brésil*), *Décor Marine*, *Décor de Pêche*, *Décor le Pont*, *Décor Pastorale*, a single large panel like an oil-painting, *Les Prodigues*(fig. 66), another large panel and *La Chasse*.

In 1863 Desfossé was joined by his brother-in-law, Hippolyte Karth, himself the successor of Dauptain (see below), another prominent wallpaper making concern which, about 1851, became Clerc et Margeridon.

Jules Desfossé died in 1889 and the "documents" etc. of the Société Desfossé et Karth became, in 1947, the property of Société Isidore Leroy.

One of the curious things about tracing the history of these wallpaper men is the way in which both artists and makers seem inevitably to attain considerable fame in the course of the years, the changes of ownership or normal succession. Thus we find Jacquemart et Bénard emerging from the Réveillon business and, a few years later, the firm is settling down

---

★ Nancy McClelland stated that this decoration, which was seen at the Paris Exposition, in 1855, was printed entirely by machine.

into a position of authority as far as fine wallpapers are concerned. S. Lapeyre (see below), succeeds Dufour with distinction and Desfossé et Karth, as we have seen, springs from a concern built up by Mader who originally worked for Dufour. There does not appear to have been anything like a manufacturers' association during the period these men were working (as there is today in France), otherwise we might have been able to turn up its records to discover how they proceeded, how they bought their paper, priced their goods and what ideas they had about standardising dimensions, advertising, etc. all of which must have assumed importance in their day. It is an aspect which deserves closer investigation, perhaps, for the early manufacturers of small decorated sheets in France are recorded as having formed themselves into an organised group two hundred years before the scenics came into being and there was a close-knit association of French furniture makers during the 18th century.

At the moment, however, we are concerned with getting as close as possible to a complete list of scenic, and near-scenic wallpapers made during the sixty, or seventy prolific years. A number (as will be seen from Appendix I), have been noted: it now remains to mention a few less well-known examples.

S. Lapeyre, with his partner Drouard, a former manager of the Dufour business, succeeded to the latter firm in 1836 and continued, under various managements until taken over, about 1865 by Desfossé et Karth. They seem not to have launched into scenic production in a big way maybe because they could see the beginning of the end of these decorations, but they did produce a "grand décor" in grisaille, entitled, *Vues d'Italie*. From what one can discover their work consisted in the main of drapery papers and "tentures en ton d'or", some of which earned the partners a certain amount of notice and at least one award at the Paris exhibitions. In 1846 they issued an ambitious decoration entitled, *Décor Chasse et Pêche*, which was given an alternative title *Renaissance*. This "grand décor", designed by Wagner, the "paysagiste", who also designed for Desfossé and other wallpaper makers, consisted of a central panel and numerous accessory borders, pilasters and cartouches which could be applied according to taste. This was, in fact, reissued by Desfossé et Karth about 1859 which shows that it must have enjoyed a fair amount of success originally. Quite early Arthur et Grenard, of Paris, had produced a decoration entitled "La Fête du Roi aux Champs Elysées" which André Carlhian said was very beautiful.

J-B. Dauptain was the founder of the business which, at the end of the 18th century was trading as "A La Renommée", at 26 Rue St Bernard, Paris. On his death his widow, and her son and daughter, carried on and, with the assistance of several experienced designers, produced all kinds of wallpaper and also a number of 'décors' including, in 1832, a composition by Portelet, entitled *Décor Grec*, an ingenious arrangement of accessory ornaments in the Desfossé tradition which had, as its name implies, a distinct classical feeling (fig. 61).*

And there was Delicourt, who won the highest award at the Great Exhibition of 1851, in London, for his tremendously impressive *Grand Chasse* (figs. 46-48), which cost more than 40,000 francs to produce. It is doubtful whether even the French wallpaper historians will be able to discover every wallpaper maker who entered the field during the first half of the 19th century. Even before the Revolution there were as many as thirty or forty

---

* Dauptain may also have produced *Décor Pompéien* in 1832.

factories busily turning out a great variety of wallpapers and by the year 1860, about which time the scenics and "grands décors" were losing their appeal, there were in Paris alone one hundred and twenty-nine "fabricants" employing some 4,500 workers including children under the age of sixteen. Considering these figures it is remarkable that such progress as this was possible in France during a half-century which saw not only a revolution of the greatest magnitude and the collapse of the soldier-Emperor's ambitions, but also the entrance and exits of successive governments which, as we have seen, did little to encourage directly the making of wallpaper.

But far from despairing about the situation it seems that not even the revolution caused any break in production (though it eliminated more than one of the industry's leading figures somewhat suddenly), and, surprisingly, many of the firms destined to come to the forefront during the Empire and later, were being set up at this time.

Other wallpaper makers who played a comparatively minor role in the development of the scenic wallpaper whose names should be mentioned are: Paul Balin (1863–98); Bezault et Pattey (1867–78); Brière; Clerc et Margeridon; and Wagner (1840–60). Cartulat (1811–1843), maker of wallpaper "pour les salles de spectacle"; Hiner (1808–); Sauvinet (1823).

# VII

# Comments

IT IS ALWAYS interesting to look into the past for comments upon subjects which specially concern us. Most historians depend upon the examination of documents, letters or memoirs to give "life" to factual information and the wallpaper historian is no exception. A letter from a lady living in 18th century London to her friend in the country provides useful evidence of decorative styles current at the time when she describes the character of a new wallpaper: " . . . the dining room is 21 ft. long by 17 ft. wide, and is to be new papered this week. The paper is to be a blue, small-patterned flock. I will send you a bit of it".★ This is the sort of thing that enlivens dry-as-dust history and, of course, it is the very stuff of which history is made.

It is not very difficult to discover past comment about wallpaper: many books have been founded on casual observation of the subject, and it is hoped that the random comments offered in the present instance may throw some light on the way it was regarded by ordinary people and also what they felt about the pictorial wallpapers we have just been discussing.

For instance, Mrs Philip Lybbe Powys, to whom so many historians turn, writes, in 1803, about a gentleman friend living in Bath, who found the Parisians' view of wallpaper so unfavourable ("vulgar" was the expression used), that on his return from a visit there he took all his papers down and hung his rooms with satin. True, this was a year or two before the advent of the first of the scenic wallpapers but it does seem possible that the smaller pictorial-type papers which preceded the larger ones—the panoramic papers—might be the ones to which the discerning would take a dislike. As we shall see there was a great division of opinion about wallpaper in general and the scenic wallpapers in particular and while some were unable to favour either, others like, for example, the Jury of the Paris Lycée des Arts, at the end of the 18th century, considered that manufacturers of paperhangings had reached a high degree of perfection and that France owed her superiority in this respect "to the study of drawing which ordinarily forms part of the education of the industrial classes and of which the knowledge has spread to the well-to-do who are the principal consumers and whose taste ultimately determines the direction which the manufacturers give to their work".

Although the comment belongs to a somewhat later date, 1826 in fact, it seems that the Rev. Sydney Smith, who so much admired bright and cheerful things, was an enthusiast of French wallpaper for he expressed his admiration of it during a visit to his beloved Paris that year. In a letter to his wife he writes: "Dearest Kate, I went yesterday into a great upholsterer's shop [unfortunately he did not name it], and nothing can exceed the magnificence of the furniture. Their papers are most beautiful that I think I shall bring some over."

---

★ Manuscripts of Lord Kenyon. Hist. MSS. Commission 14th Report.

This he did and Sydney Smith, being the adventurous, enquiring fellow he was, must surely have included a scenic set among his purchases. If indeed this was the case one wonders which of the scenic sets, by this time available in great variety, he would have chosen and did he, by chance, have a note of the dimensions of the room at home which he proposed to decorate in this way? All this is fairly reasonable assumption as his superlatives seem to confirm that the wallpapers were very much out of the ordinary.

Another literary figure, Honoré de Balzac, held an entirely opposite view and while his contemporary, Théophile Gautier, concedes the scenic paper to be "a useful encyclopaedia to study while waiting for the soup", the author of *Le Père Goriot* (1834), is far from complimentary. Describing the dining room of a small Parisian boarding house he considers nothing could be more sad than this room with its faded furniture and its scenic wallpaper, "un papier verni" (varnished), which for many years had been the subject of ribald jokes by those who lodged there. The paper in question was the one which was called *Les Paysages de Télémaque dans l'Ile de Calypso* (see Chapter V).★

As has been seen (fig. 28/29), the subject was a very beautiful one and Balzac's comment can only be accounted for by the fact that the French aesthete, like his English counterpart, was not in favour of imitation and looked upon the scenic wallpaper (so similar to decorative painting), as coming within this despised category. We shall return to the vexed question of imitation in a few moments: in the meantime perhaps the view of a prominent Parisian industrialist is not without interest. It has been stated that in 1830 useful notes on the manufacture of wallpaper were published by one Sebastien Le Normand, a friend of the famous maker, Joseph Dufour. The latter produced all kinds of wallpaper but it is of the scenic variety that Le Normand writes: "M. Dufour", he states, "is one of the best wallpaper manufacturers [in Paris], and deserves great praise for the work he is pursuing with so much perfection." He then proceeds, as we have seen, to explain ways of hanging two of the better known scenic sets. There is no diffidence in these notes, no doubts as to the propriety of the pictorial character of the scenic paper: rather there is unqualified acceptance and confident assurance. So it is for a less biased opinion that we turn to the Englishman, Richard Redgrave, R.A. one of the Jurors of the Great Exhibition of 1851 who was subsequently entrusted with the task of criticising the wallpaper design exhibited.

It is a lengthy report containing a good deal of Victorian verbiage yet it is worth while dealing with it in some detail seeing that in addition to its general condemnation of imitative effects it also deals generally with the scenic wallpaper topic, and with one such specifically.

The first paragraphs describe what the writer feels should be the purpose of a wallhanging whether paper or textile. Is it, he asks, to enrich the general effect of a room, temper the heat of summer or give a sense of warmth and comfort to the winter? Is it required to increase or decrease the size of a room? And so forth until, at last, out comes what he really wishes to say: " . . . the design of a decoration should be flat and conventionalised, and lines and forms, harsh or cutting on the ground, as far as possible avoided. Imitative treatments are objectionable on principle both as intruding on the sense of flatness and as being too attractive

---

★ Balzac also disliked the scenic paper called, *Le Paysage Turc* in the dining room of his "vielle fille", Mlle Gamard of Tours·

in their details and colour to be sufficiently retiring and unobtrusive." What chance did a French scenic paper stand in the face of such a dictum?

Mr Redgrave continues, "But it is everywhere apparent that the combination of many colours though it may increase the expense from the number of blocks, is far from producing richness in the same degree, while it has quite often the contrary effect and results only in poverty and meanness." (Some of the larger scenics, of course, contained as many as 80–100 colours.) Anything (especially wallpaper), which contained realistic ornament such as architectural features, pilasters, *picture compositions*, statues, fruits or flowers, skilfully drawn and printed though they might be, was just a sham, "amenable to no laws and necessarily false in light and shade, often constructively inapplicable and always impertinent and obtrusive and should be left to those who, desiring display, are too much wanting in taste to be annoyed at its truth and extravagance!"

When he dealt with the scenic wallpapers he naturally singled out the one which had been featured prominently in the Exhibition, the astonishing panoramic wallpaper produced by the Parisian manufacturer, Etienne Delicourt entitled *La Grande Chasse*. It has been mentioned in the last chapter but suffice it to say this decoration, issued in 16 lengths, called for the use of 4,000 blocks in its printing. It was made from paintings by an artist, well thought of at the time, called Antoine Dury and was considered by some to hold its own with many works of fine art. "Elle est capable de s'élever aux plus beaux effets de l'art". Redgrave could not have disagreed more.

Then, the *Art Journal*, always observant of the fads and fancies of the world of art during the 19th century, often cast a critical eye on the applied arts, or the "art industries" as they were called, and in 1861 a writer by the name of John Stewart composed a well-informed and critical series of articles on French and English wallpapers. In these articles he listed reasons for the French makers' superiority in this field most of which merited serious consideration seeing that the author had undertaken a number of visits to factories in both countries. Firstly the colours and the colourists in France were superior;* then the French not only treated their designers as artists of standing but paid them more for their designs; the French generally used more expensive materials than the English and they paid their workmen more.

Delicourt's admirable approach to wallpaper manufacture was mentioned in support of these arguments and with some reason, for among the French paperstainers of the day this particular firm was in the first rank. "If he wants a group of flowers or anything from that up to a great *pictorial picture*", Stewart writes: "He [the French manufacturer], will employ a first rate artist to paint them in oil as pictures, and buy them at picture prices. He will then employ another artist who understands the 'mechanique' of the trade to convert these pictures into patterns, for as each block must print a flat tint a picture must be translated by the designer before it can be cut into blocks, and some of these translators are themselves high class artists. It is in this process of translation that Delicourt seems to stand before all his compères."

---

* An English decorator of distinction, John Gregory Crace, in a lecture to the R.I.B.A., in 1839, also admitted that the French then had a better eye for colour than the English.

This comment, because of its frankness, evoked a spirited, but not very convincing, reply from an English manufacturer who used a Manchester newspaper as a vehicle for his indignation but would no doubt take some of the censures to heart.

There was another Great Exhibition in London, this time in 1862, and once again the French came in for a lot of praise despite the fact that some of the most eminent English manufacturers were arrayed against them: but this time the praise contained a nagging doubt about the great panoramic-type decorations which were most likely losing something of their magic by now. Richard Redgrave had, perhaps, hit the nail on the head in 1851. While admitting that *La Grande Chasse* was "powerfully executed and skilfully blocked" he reiterated his firm opinion that pictorial treatments "were wrong whenever they intruded on the domains of another art".

The *Illustrated London News* held the same view of one of the scenic papers in the 1862 exhibition.* This is what it had to say: " . . . but while this is a work of great magnificence it must suffer condemnation if it is regarded as the decoration of a wall. A picture is a scene viewed as a landscape through a window, but a picture the size of a wall without any margin or frame would not be very pleasing; it needs a boundary, and is unsuited as a background, both through its obtrusiveness and the fact that it is altogether inconsistent to hide parts with articles of furniture. Indeed we could not afford to do so; for what part of a composition could be spared? Were this a suitable background the manufacturer would have papered his screen with a landscape, and have hung the other works exhibited upon it; but instead of so doing he prepares the screen with a low-toned maroon ground, and borders the picture with a massive frame, the bold aspect of which is curiously heightened by false shade which is added."

It is not difficult to imagine the rivalry which these recurring international exhibitions occasioned. Although the idea of competing with the French on their "panoramique" ground, as it were, probably filled the English manufacturer with apprehension, these big exhibitions made demands upon his ingenuity which it was difficult to resist. His attempts to compete in this field, however, did not amount to very much unless in the way of certain "novelties" like, for instance, the colourful "pilaster" designs requiring rather more block-cutting than was usual (fig. 67), and also a frieze 24 ft. in length, consisting of selected portions of the Elgin Marbles. It seems a pity that no photograph or print was made of this last masterpiece so that posterity might compare the treatment of this classical subject with that of, say, Dufour's *Galerie Mythologique* (fig. 18). There is no doubt that the French would have emerged from such a comparison with flying colours, for their supremacy in this kind of work was everywhere acknowledged right through the 60's after which public demand veered towards simpler effects.†

---

* This was a scenic paper made by Jules Desfossé. It may have been *L'Eden* produced about 1860 ." . . . a compilation of the beauties of many lands; plants from varied countries . . . on the one side a cedar in spring leafage; on the other a Virginian creeper in autumn foliage and these are combined with the bigonia, the strelitzia, and other plants" (fig. 56).

† Sir Charles Oman writes in *Memories of Victorian Oxford* published in 1941, " . . . Old Mrs Myers had a classical Georgian house which had been built for the exiled heir of the Bourbons, the Duc de Berri about 1808 . . . The interior of the house was pure French 'Empire', there was one room papered with a gorgeous view of the Tuileries Gardens under the 'ancien régime' with ladies and soldiers promenading . . . a favourite decoration scheme of the time. I often wondered how so much French wallpaper could have been smuggled over to England about the time of the Napoleonic Wars."

Mention has been made of the popularity of these papers in America. In her book, *Historic Wallpapers*, Nancy McClelland explained that when the French scenics first became known in America the two countries were enjoying a close relationship as a result of the war with England during which French and American blood had been shed in a common cause. What was done by the French set the fashion for America and so in this way many sets of these decorations found their way into American homes where they may still be seen today. She wrote: "Often they were brought into the country as wedding gift or birthday or anniversary present by some sea captain specially charged with their transportation. The paper was carried across the ocean in its original small sheets, these being sometimes wrapped in tinfoil tubes to protect them from the dampness of the sea trip. Each sheet was numbered and when they reached their destination they were put together on the walls with the aid of a chart after the fashion of children's picture puzzles. Very few scenic papers found their way below the Mason and Dixon line: they mostly stayed in, or near, the Northern seaport owns where they landed. To the dwellings of the old New Englanders they brought a riot of colour that appeared almost licentious after the severity of white-washed walls. They filled the rooms with movement, romance and light."

Nancy McClelland went on to state that at the time of writing (1924) it was estimated there were over 200 examples of these scenic papers to be found in America but that only just over half of these had actually been seen and much fewer than this number identified. This statement obviously made in good faith, appears to conflict with the views of other equally reliable authorities notably M. Robert Carlhian, son of the late André Carlhian, who informed the writer that, in all, about 110 different scenic papers were printed between 1805 and 1865, the year when their popularity had begun to wane.

It is impossible to close any catalogue of comment on the scenic wallpaper without referring to Henri Clouzot's remarks which appear in his Foreword to Nancy McClelland's book mentioned above:

"The manufacturers have succeeded, at the cost of what amazing efforts, in imitating painting with wallpaper, with all its effects of light and shade, of colour and perspective. Dufour, Leroy, Zuber, in spite of their masterpieces, fall into the error of Oudry (the 18th century artist), when he directed tapestry, sixty years earlier, towards the servile reproduction of painting. Painting is one thing: wallpaper is another. Even in grisaille, where the general tonality is a note of harmonious half-tones, scenic paper is apt to count too much in a room. It attracts interest when it should serve only as an accompaniment.

Let us say, however, in defence of the decorators of the beginning of the 19th century, that the dwellings of that day contained much less furniture than ours. Certain rooms, like entrance halls, had none whatever . . .

If these panels, when they are the work of a Laffitte, like the story of Psyche, are worthy of the dwelling of an artist, the scenes of Telemachus in the Island of Calypso are proper to put in the bourgeois boarding house of Madame Vauquier and to frame the ludicrous face of Père Goriot."

And M. Clouzot adds the warning:

"Do not confuse the interest of curiosity which inspires us today with the admiration reserved for real works of art."

# TITLES OF SCENIC WALLPAPERS COMPILED FROM VARIOUS SOURCES

*Amours de Psyche; Les*, Psyche et Cupidon, Le Bain de Psyche, Amor und Psyche (Dufour).

*d'Anthenor; Les Voyages*, Reisen des Anthenor (Dufour).

*l'Arcadie;* Arkadische Landschaften, Arkadie (Zuber).

*l'Amerique du Nord; Les Vues de*, Ansichten von Nordamerika (see also "War of Independence") (Zuber).

*d'Austerlitz; La Bataille*, Die Schlacht von Austerlitz, 1814.

*Asiatiques; Les Vues*, Chinesische Landschaften (Unknown).

*Arabe; Le Camp*, Araber-Zeltlager (Unknown).

*d'Armide; Le Jardin*, Gärten der Armide (Desfossé et Karth).

*Aneis-Tapete* (Dufour).

*Armées Francaises en Italie; Campagnes des*, Napoleon in Italien (Dufour).


*Bosphore; Les Rives du*, Die Ufer des Bosporus (Dufour).

*Bagatelle; Le Jardin de*, Jardins Francais, ?Le Petit Decor, Der Gärten Bagatelle (Zuber).

*Brésil; Vues du*, Brasilianische Landschaften, Ansichten von Brasilien (Zuber).

*Bonheur; Rêve de*, Der Traum vom Gluck (Desfossé et Karth).

*Brésil; Le* (Defossé et Karth).

*Boucher; Tapisserie* (Unknown).

*Baujon; b. Neuilly; Jardin*, (Mit einer Rutschbahn) (Unknown).


*Chasse; Paysages à*, Landschaft mit Jagden (Zuber).

*Chinois; le Décor* (Zuber).

*Chevaux; Les Courses de*, Die Pferderennen (Zuber).

*Compiègne; La Chasse de*, Die Jagd von Compiègne (Jacquemart et Bénard).

*Cloud; Saint-, Les Jardins* (Unknown).

*Champs Elysées; La Fête du Roi, aux*, Das Fest des Konigs (Arthur et Guenard).

*Chemin de Fer de Saint-Etienne*, Die Eisenbahn nach St-Etienne (Pignet St Genis-Laval).

*Chinois; Panorama* (Desfossé et Karth).

*Chasseurs Ecossais; Les* (Mader).

*Chasse; La* (Desfossé et Karth).

*Chasse et Pêche: Décor*, (Lapeyere).


*Détroits; l'Ouverture des*, Offnung der Dardanellen (Unknown).


*Espagnole; Les Jardins*, Spanische Gärten ?Le Jardin de Bagatelle (see above) (Zuber).

*d'Ecosse; Vues*, Lady of the Lake, Ansichten von Schottland, Die Frau am Meer (Zuber).

*El Dorado* (Zuber).
*Egypte; Les Français en*, Die Französen in Agypten (Dufour).
*l'Eden*, Der Gärten Eden (Desfossé et Karth).
*Ernten; Die* (Pignet St Genis-Laval).
*Exotische Landschaft* (perhaps "Le Brésil") (Desfossé et Karth).
*Essling; Schlacht bei*, 1809 (Unknown).
*l'Empire; Fastes Glorieux de* (mentioned by Carlhian) (Unknown).

*Fêtes Grecques; Les*, Griechische Feste (see Olympic Fetes) (Dufour).
*Fables; Paysages à*, Die Fabellandschaften (see Décor à Fables) (Zuber).
*France; Les Ports de*, Französische Häfen, um 1800 (Unknown).
*Fleurs; Les Saisons des*, Die Jahreszeiten der Blumen (Desfossé et Karth).
*Français; Parc* (Jacquemart et Bénard).
*France Mâcon; Le Décor* (Desfossé et Karth).

*Grèce Moderne; Les Vues de la*, ou le Combat des Grecs. Freiheitskämpfe der Griechen (Zuber).
*Grande Chasse; La*, Die Grösse Jagd (Delicourt).
*Grec: Décor* (Dauptain).
*Glorieuses: Les Trois* (mentioned by Carlhian) (Unknown).
*Guerre de l'Indépendence Italienne.*

*l'Helvétie;* La Grande Helvétie, Helvetien Oder, Die Grösse Schweiz (see also William Tell) (Zuber).
*Huguenots; Les*, Die Hugenotten (Pignet St Genis-Laval).
*d'Hiver; Le Jardin*, Der Wintergarten (Desfossé et Karth).
*Heimkehr von der Heuernte*, 1820 (Unknown).

*Indische Landschaft* (Dufour).
*Italienische Stadtansichten* (Unknown).
*Incas; Les*, ou la Destruction de l'Empire du Pérou, Die Inkas (Dufour).
*d'Italie; Les Vues*, ou la Baie de Naples, Bay of Naples, Ansichten von Italien (Dufour).
*l'Indoustan;* Indische Landschaft (Zuber).
*d'Italie; Vues*, Italienische Landschaft (Zuber).
*Independence; War of*, La Guerre de l'Indépendence (see also "l'Amerique du Nord") (Zuber).
*Isola Bella* (Zuber).
*d'Italie; La Revolution* (Zuber).
*l'Inde; Vues de*, Ansichten von Indien (Zuber).
*d'Italie; Vues* (Lapeyere).

*Japonais; Paysage*, Japanische Landschaft (Zuber).
*Japonais; Décor à Personnages*, Japanische mit Figurlichen (see above) (Unknown).
*Joseph; Histoire*, Josefslegende (Unknown).
*La Jeunesse 1855*, Die Jugend (Delicourt).

*Lointains; Les*, Ferne Landschaften (Zuber).
*Lyon; Les Vues de*, Ansichten von Lyon (Sauvinet, Paris or Pignet de Saint Genis-Laval).
*Louis XIII; Les Fêtes* (see Champs Elysées) (Unknown).
*Louis XIII; Chasse sous* (Unknown).
*Louis XVI; Décor* (Unknown).

*Mer Pacifique; Les Paysages de la*, Les Sauvages de la Mer Pacifique, Captain Cook, Reisen des Kapitän Cook (Dufour).
*Monuments de Paris; Les* (Dufour).
*Mexico; La Conquête, du*, Die Eroberung von Mexiko (Zuber).
*Maritime Directoire; Le Paysage*, Kustenlandschaft, um 1795–99 (Robert).
*Métamorphoses; Les* (Unknown).
*Mediterranéens; Les Rivages*, Die Mittelmeerküste (Unknown).
*Militaires; Scènes*, Militärische Bilder (Pignet St Genis-Laval).
*Moderne; Décor*, Moderner Dekor 1925 (Desfossé et Karth).
*Molière Tapete* (Mader).
*Mythologique; La Galerie*, Mythologische Galerie (Dufour).
*Mois; Les Douze*, The Twelve Months, Monate; Die 12 (Dufour).
*Marine; Dekor* (Desfossé et Karth).

*Néo-Grec; Décor* (Monuments de Paris; not really a scenic) (Desfossé et Karth).

*Olympic; Fêtes*, Olympische Feste (see Fêtes Grècques) (Desfossé et Karth).
*d'Océanie; Archipels* (mentioned by Carlhian) (Unknown).

*Paul et Virginie;* Paul und Virginie (Dufour).
*Pittoresque; Paysage* (Dufour).
*Palais Royal; Les Jardins du*, Gärten des Palais Royal (Unknown).
*Pêche et Chasse*, Fischen und Jagen (Lapeyere).
*Paris, Londres, Rome* (Pignet St Genis-Laval).
*Pêche; Dekor de* (Desfossé et Karth).
*Pont; Dekor le* (Desfossé et Karth).
*Poetique; La Galerie* (Desfossé et Karth).
*Pastorale: Décor* (Desfossé et Karth).
*Les Prodigues* (Desfossé et Karth).

*Quichotte; Don*, Les Aventures (Unknown).
*Quatre Ages de la Vie*, Die vier Lebensalter (Unknown).

*Renaud et Armide*, Renaud und Armide (Dufour).
*Romain; La Campagne* (Unknown).
*Roland Furieux, ou Angélique et Médor*, Der rasende Roland nach Ariost (Unknown).
*Révolution de Paris*, 1830 (Unknown).

*Rivière; Les Bords de la,* Küsten an der Riviera (Unknown).
*Révolutionnaires; Scènes* (Unknown).
*Romanische Szenen* (Pignet St Genis-Laval).
*Rom; Ruine de,* Romische Ruinen, um 1800 (Unknown).
*Rom; Ansichten von,* um 1800 (Unknown).
*Renaissance* (see "Décor Chasse et Pêche") (Lapeyere).

*Suisse; Les Vues de,* Schweizer Ansichten (Zuber).
*Siciliennes; Scènes,* Sizilianische Bilder (Zuber).
*Saisons; Les Quatre,* Die vier Jahrezeiten (Jacquemart et Bénard).
*Spanische Landschaft* (possibly Jacquemart et Bénard).
*Säulen von Athen* (Dufour).

*Télémaque dans l'île de Calypso; Paysages de,* Abenteuer des Telemach (Dufour).
*Tell; Guillaume* (see l'Helvetie "Vues de Suisse", etc.) (Zuber).
*Terrestre; Les Zones,* Die Zonen der Erde (Zuber).
*Téniers; Tapisserie* (Unknown).
*Türkische Landschaft* (Dufour).
*Tuileries; l'Attaque du Louvre et des* (mentioned by Carlhian) (Unknown).

*Vernet; Chasses de,* Die Jagd nach Vernet (Delicourt).
*Versailles; Château de* (Unknown).
*Villefranche; Côtes de,* Kustenlandschaft (Zuber).
*Ville: Les Plaisirs de la, et de la Campagne,* Vergnügen in Stadt und Land (Unknown).
*Venise; Les Vues de,* Ansichten von Venedig (Unknown).
*Venus; Toilette de* (ceiling decoration) (Dufour).

# AUTHORITIES CONSULTED

Art Journal, The
Bohn's Pictorial Handbook of London
(Honoré de Balzac) Le Père Goriot
(Carlhian, André) Notes
(Clouzot, Henri and Follot, Charles) Histoire du Papier Peint. 1935
Connoisseur, The
Country Life
(Decorators Handbook) Paperhanger, Painter, etc. 1878
Dictionnaire de Biographie Français
(Follot, F.) Causerie sue le Papier Peint. 1886
(Figuier, Louis) Merveilles de l'Industrie. 1878
Illustrated London News
(McClelland, Nancy) Historic Wallpapers. 1924
(Normand, Sebastien le) Manuel des Étoffes, etc. 1886
(Oman, C. C.) Catalogue of Wallpaper. 1929. Victoria and Albert Museum
(Sanborn, Kate) Old Time Wallpapers. 1905
Science, Magazine of
(Seguin, J-P) Le Papier Peint en France. 1968
(Sugden, A. V. and Edmondson, J. L.) History of English Wallpaper. 1926
Tapeten, Ihre Geschichte Bis Zur Gegenwart. 1970
Tapet-Nyatt (Norway) November 1964. Article by G. Tilander

# INDEX

1. (left) Chinese landscape paper—part of a continuous picture. 96 in. × 46½ in. 18th century.
*Courtesy, Victoria and Albert Museum, London*

2. (right) Réveillon. Arabesque panel "Coq et Perroquet", 1785. Printed in distemper by wood blocks on sheets of vellum pasted together to form a roll about 5–6 ft. Designed by Jean-Baptiste Fay.
*Courtesy, Musée des Arts Décoratifs, Paris*

3. (top) John Baptist Jackson (1701–77). An example of his chiaro-oscuro, wood engraved, productions about 20 in. square. Mid 18th century.

4. (bottom) Sir James Thornhill (1675–1734). Scheme for a mural design for a large room.
*Both courtesty, Victoria and Albert Museum*

5. An "over-door" decoration by Arthur et Robert, Paris, *c.* 1786. About 2 ft. × 3 ft.
*Courtesy, Musée des Arts Décoratifs, Paris*

6. (left) Wallpaper printed by Réveillon of Paris used as a book cover, 1792.

7. (right) Revolutionary Panel, probably by Jacquemart et Bénard. Similar to many used in the offices of the administration. Late 18th century.
*Courtesy, Musée des Arts Décoratifs, Paris*

8. (left) "Les Deux Pigeons" printed by Réveillon "Royal Manufacturer" of Paris. Late 18th century. Printed in coloured flock on a spotted ground.
*Courtesy, Victoria and Albert Museum*

9. (right) Hand printed paper by Zuber of Rixheim, *c.* 1843. Part of a set.

10. (top) "La Jetée", a cameo probably by Amable Leroy, *c.* 1828. About 2 ft. × 3 ft.

11. (bottom) "Scène de Naufrage" another cameo decoration attributed to Le Veuve Mader, *c.* 1830. About 2 ft. × 3 ft. For use as screens, "supraportes" or overmantels.
*Both courtesy, Musée des Arts Décoratifs, Paris*

12. A wallpaper of conventional design by Jacquemart et Bénard, *c.* 1760–80.
*Courtesy,* Musée des Arts Décoratifs, *Paris*

13. (top) Over–door decoration, *c.* 1840. Maker not known

14. (bottom) The so-called Molière panels produced *c.* 1825 by Mader.
*Both courtesy, Deutsches Tapeten Museum, Kassel*

15. One of a set of "The Twelve Months" printed in grisaille by Dufour et Leroy, 1808. Each panel about 3 ft. × 18 in. Designs attributed to Evariste Fragonard (1780–1850).

16. Dufour et Leroy. Three lengths of the famous twenty-piece set titled "Les Sauvages de la Mer Pacifique", often referred to as the Captain Cook wallpaper. Printed 1806. Original paintings by Jean Gabriel Charvet.

17. (top) "Les Jeunes Artistes", imitation panelling produced by Bezault et Pattey Fils in 1867.

18. (bottom) Dufour et Leroy. Panel from "La Galerie Mythologique" designed by Xavier Mader, 1814. The set comprises twenty-four lengths each about 4 ft. × 18 in. wide. Printed in grisaille.
*Both courtesy, Musée des Arts Décoratifs, Paris*

19. Dufour et Leroy "Renaud et Armide". First printed 1828. Part of a thirty-two length set. Possibly the last scenic wallpaper supervised by Dufour. The scene is entitled "The Enchanted Forest".
*Courtesy, Musée des Arts Décoratifs, Paris*

20. "Les Amours de Psyche" or "Psyche and Cupid". Four of the twenty-six lengths of this beautiful decoration designed by Louis Laffitte and produced by Dufour in 1816. This tableau is titled "Psyche shows her jewels to her sisters".
*In the Whitworth Art Gallery, Manchester*

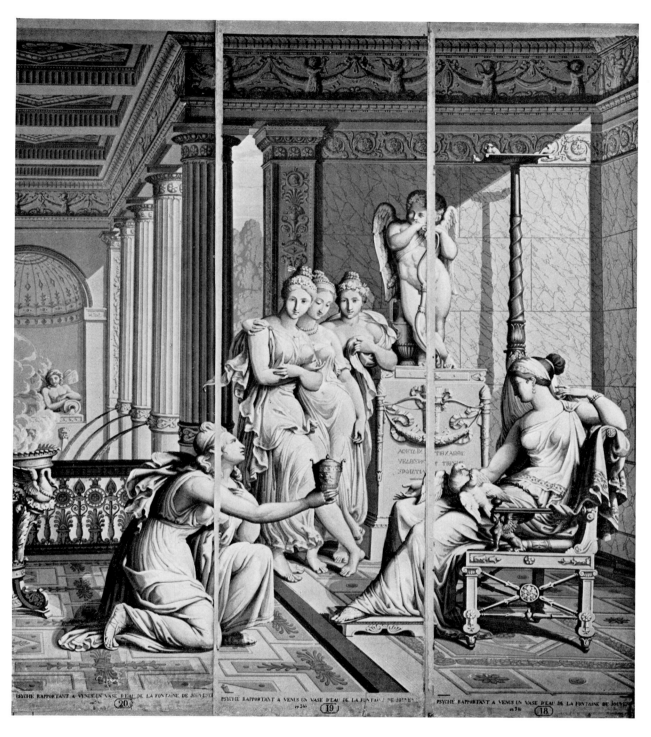

21. Dufour et Leroy "Les Amours de Psyche". Three more lengths of this set depicting Psyche presenting to Venus a vase containing water from the Fountain of Youth.

*In the Whitworth Gallery, Manchester*

22. Dufour et Leroy "Les Amours de Psyche". Three further lengths entitled the "Reconciliation of Psyche and Venus".
*In the Whitworth Art Gallery, Manchester*

23/24. Dufour et Leroy. Four more lengths, two panels, illustrating further events in the Psyche legend.
*In the Whitworth Art Gallery, Manchester*

25/26. Dufour et Leroy "Les Incas". Tableau from this magnificent twenty-five length set depicting scenes from the book by Marmontel recounting the Conquest of Peru by Pizarro. Dufour produced this decoration in 1826.

27. Dufour et Leroy "Les Incas". One of the tableaux entitled "An Inca Family". Twenty-five lengths in colour called for no fewer than 2,112 blocks.

28/29. Dufour et Leroy. This twenty-five length production "Paysages de Télémaque dans l'Ile de Calypso" was issued in 1825. Balzac's novel *Le Père Goriot* (1834) refers to this set rather disparagingly.

30. Dufour et Leroy "Les Monuments de Paris" a thirty-length decoration designed by Mader and produced by Dufour about 1814. In this section the Arc de Carrousel is seen in the centre panel.
*Courtesy, Victoria and Albert Museum*

31/32. Dufour et Leroy "Les Monuments de Paris". Further scenes from this truly panoramic decoration.
*Courtesy, Victoria and Albert Museum*

33. Three lengths of a spectacular decoration entitled "Vues de l'Inde". Believed to have been produced by Dufour in 1815.

34. (left) "Les Jardins Francais". Produced by Zuber in 1821 from a design by Mongin.

35. (right) Zuber "Vues de l'Amérique du Nord". First issued *c.* 1834–6. This section depicts the Niagara Falls.

36. The French Campaigns in Egypt. A set of thirty-two lengths. Designed by Deltil and produced by Dufour
et Leroy, *c.* 1814 or earlier.

37/38. Zuber "Vues de l'Amérique du Nord". Two further scenes from this interesting decoration
—includng views of Boston Harbour.

39. French Campaign in Egypt—the base of the column (left) inscribed "The 20th March 1800, 10,000 French under the brave Kléber conquered 80,000 Turks in the plains of Heliopolis". Produced *c.* 1814.
*Courtesy, Cooper Union Museum, New York*

40. Zuber "Les Vues de Brésil". First issued *c.* 1829. A dramatic scene from
this decoration designed by Rugendas.
*Courtesy, Musée des Arts Décoratifs, Paris*

41/42. Zuber "La Dame du Lac" or "Vues d'Écosse". Scenes from this thirty-two length decoration, probably designed by J. Michel Gué (1789–1843) and issued by Zuber et Cie, *c.* 1827. This set is unusual in that it was printed in two separate shades of grisaille, dark greys for the trees and sepias for the figures. Zuber also printed a special gothic dado paper to go with it.

*Courtesy, Lennox Money Ltd., London, S.W.1*

43/44. Zuber "La Dame du Lac". Further scenes from this set, believed to be inspired by a novel by Walter Scott. Each length measures 7 or 8 ft. long and about 18 in. wide.

*Courtesy, Lennox Money Ltd., London, S.W.1*

45. "La Jeunesse". Designed by Charles L. Muller and produced in 1855 by Fabrique d'Etienne Delicourt.

46/47/48. Delicourt "La Grande Chasse". This decoration after designs by François Desportes, part of which is here illustrated, was shown at the Great Exhibition of 1851. No fewer than 4,000 blocks were used. Fig. 46/47 (top) show the order of hanging the lengths.

*Courtesy, Musée des Arts Décoratifs, Paris*

49/50. Zuber *c.* 1825. "Décor Chinois". This decoration is well known in France, Germany and America. The illustration shown here appeared in *Country Life* (23rd November, 1951). The identity of the lower picture is uncertain though it may be part of "Décor Chinois".

51. Dufour et Leroy "Les Portique d'Athènes". One panel from a set
believed to be so-named.
*Courtesy Cooper Union Museum, New York*

52/53. Dufour et Leroy "Les Vues d'Italie" or "The Bay of Naples", *c.* 1822–24. Printed in monochrome tints of varying colour. This decoration was issued in thirty-three lengths.

54. Dufour et Leroy "Les Vues d'Italie". Enlarged section of this decoration shown on the left of the doorway in Fig. 53.

55. Desfossé et Karth produced this spectacular decoration and called it "Un Rêve de Bonheur". It was designed by an artist named Durrant in 1852 and supplied with accessory decorations such as pilasters, borders, etc. as shown.
*Courtesy, Musée des Arts Décoratifs, Paris*

56. Another Desfossé et Karth production, "L'Eden" issued *c.* 1860. The drawing of the luxuriant vegetation and its translation to wood block printing is superb and typical of French expertise in this form of production.
*Courtesy, Musée des Arts Décoratifs, Paris*

57. Desfossé et Karth "Jardin d'Armide". This decoration was composed by Charles Muller, *c.* 1854. Produced in full colour it is difficult to believe that such an elaborately finished set could have been produced by wallpaper processes current at the time.

*Courtesy, Musée d'Art Décoratifs, Paris*

58 (top) Desfossé et Karth "Le Jardin d'Hiver", *c.* 1853. Another Charles Muller masterpiece in full colours issued with borders and other wallpaper accessories.
*Courtesy, Musée des Arts Décoratifs, Paris*

59. (bottom) Desfossé et Karth "Monuments de Paris". Produced *c.* 1857 sometimes known as "Décor Neo-Grec".
*Courtesy, Musée des Arts Décoratifs, Paris*

60. Characteristic arabesque decoration favoured by the great Réveillon of Paris, *c.* 1780.
*In the Round Room, Moccas Court, Herefordshire*

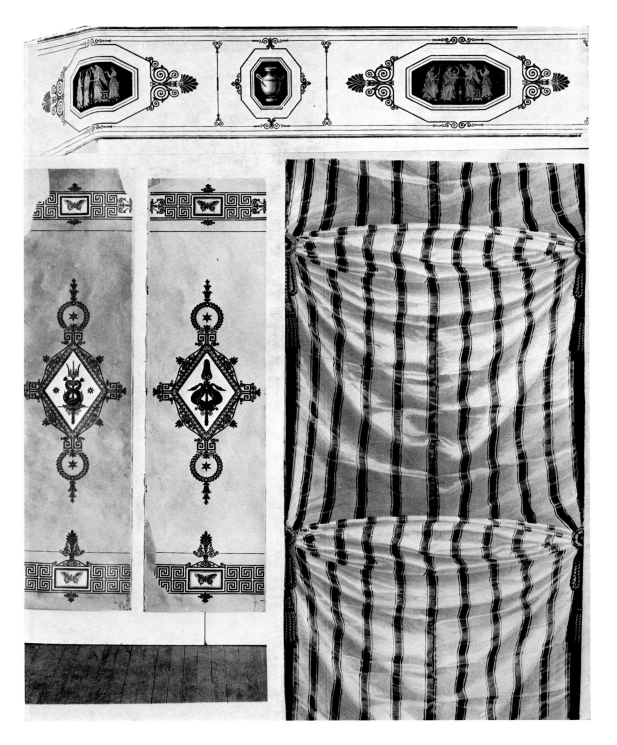

61. (top and left) Dauptain. Frieze and panels printed by this maker, c. 1832.
*Courtesy, Musée des Arts Décoratifs, Paris*

62. (right) Dufour et Leroy. Drapery design, c. 1808. Imitation of folded silk. Green stripes on white ground. About 5 ft. × 20 in. wide.
*Courtesy, Musée des Arts Décoratifs, Paris*

63. Mader. Six trophies, *c.* 1825. Each panel about 7 ft. × 2 ft. wide. Printed in bronze and gold. Medallions in white on blue in imitation of Sèvres china.
*Courtesy, Musée des Arts Décoratifs, Paris*

64. Jacquemart et Bénard "La Chasse de Compiègne". Part of a magnificent set illustrating
a Stag hunt near the Château de Compiègne. *c.* 1816.
*Courtesy, Victoria and Albert Museum, London*

65. (top) Another scenic decoration, *c.* 1816, similar to the landscape treatment of fig. 64.

66. (bottom) Desfossé et Karth, 1862. "Les Prodigues" after a painting by Thomas Couture.
*Courtesy, Victoria and Albert Museum, London*

67. Design (not put into production), *c.* 1810. View of a garden seen through pilasters and formal balustrade.
*Courtesy, Musée des Arts Décoratifs, Paris*

68. (left) Desfossé et Karth. Floral decoration of sculptured pediment designed by Charles Muller. Each motif about 7 ft. × 2 ft. wide.
*Courtesy, Musée des Arts Décoratifs, Paris*

69. (right) Zuber "L'Impératrice Eugénie", 1865. Portrait in grisaille in a framework of flowers by Gueritte. About 6 ft. × 4 ft. wide.
*Courtesy, Musée des Arts Décoratifs, Paris*